Questions for Exam Practice NY

Surviving Chemistry Regents Exam

One Day at a Time

30 Days of Practice Question Sets

for The New York State Chemistry Regents Exam

The Physical Setting

With Answers and Explanations

Regents 2012 Ready

Effiong Eyo

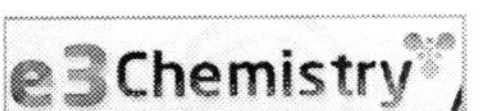

E3 Scholastic Publishing

Dedication

To my wife , Felicia. Thanks for sticking it out with me and for everything else you do.

Acknowledgement

To all the students I had the honor of teaching for twelve and a half years at Our Lady of Lourdes Catholic High School . Thank you.

ISBN-13: 978-0983132981

ISBN-10: 0983132984

Printed in the United States of America

Format of this book

This book contains sets of Chemistry Regents exam practice questions organized into days. There are a total of 30 days of question sets. Question sets are grouped into two major categories that are listed below.

Multiple Choices: Questions for Part A and B-1 practice.

There are 13 days of question sets in this category. Practice questions in this category test your ability to answer all types of multiple choice questions.

Constructed Response: Questions for Part B-2 and C practice.

There are 13 days of question sets in this category. Practice questions in this category vary from setting up problems, reading paragraphs , drawing and graphing.

Along two Regents practice exams, there are more than six Regents exams worth of multiple choice questions available for practice in this book. And there are almost five exams worth of Free Response questions available for practice in this book.

The small number of questions in each set allows for the benefits to you:

1. To quickly do a few questions, correct them, and see the result and your performance right away. You do not have to wait to complete one whole exam as with other books.

2. To make you feel less overwhelm in preparing for your Regents exam so you can study and practice more often.

Answers and Explanations

Answers are given to all questions in this book. Answer explanations are given to all questions (except for the practice exams) . Unlike many other books, this book ***does not just explain why*** the answer given to a question is the correct one. Instead, with the cleanest, clearest, most simplified, and easiest-to-follow steps ever seen, this book ***shows you how to pick out key information*** from a question and ***how to think through the question*** to arrive at the correct answer given. This method of explanations offers you a more quality review and understanding of the chemistry concept tested, and a better opportunity to answer similar questions correctly. It is highly recommended that you read up and study the steps given in the explanations to questions that you did not get correct.

Keeping Track of Points and Progress

At the end of each question set, you are provided with a space to note the number of correct points after grading. This is a very important, often overlooked, element in preparing for a test like this. By making a note of your points after each set:

. You'll be able to easily see and keep track of your progress and improvement from one multiple choice (or Free Response) set to the next.

. You'll be able to easily see and track which category of questions you are doing great on, and which category you are struggling with

. You'll be to see if what you are doing is getting you better prepared for the exam as the exam date draws near

It is almost pointless to study day-after-day without knowing whether your studying and effort are getting you better prepared for the test. This book allows you to quickly and easily keep track of your points, which allows you to see progress, improvement, and readiness for your Chemistry Regents Exam.

Preparing for your Chemistry Regents Exam

Months, weeks, and days before the Exam

Pay attention and listen to your teacher.

Your teacher knows you better than authors of exams prep books.
Pay attention in class, do what she or he says and recommends.

Attend Review Sessions.

Bring specific questions on concepts that you need the most help with. You'll get more out of a review session if your questions to specific problems are answered.

Practice Exam Quality Questions: Use This Book.

Start early (a month or so) and practice a set of questions a day at a time.
Correct your answers and read up on explanations.
Keep note of points of each set to track your progress and improvement.

Study notes and review packages

Focus your studying on concepts you have problems with because you may not have enough time to study everything.
Make notes of concepts that are not clear, and bring them to your teacher.

Alternate between studying and practicing questions. It is highly recommended that you spend a little more time time practicing questions and a little less time reading books and studying review packages.

Familiarize yourself with the current exam and scoring formats

The two full Practice Exams on Day 27 – 30 in this book are based on the most current Chemistry Regents exam format. The grading formats for all multiple choice questions and short answer questions are all based on the most current formats. Being aware of these formats is a very important element in preparing for Chemistry Regents Exam.

Night before the exam

Get a good night sleep, Relax!

Day of the exam

Eat a good meal. Relax!
Bring pencils, pens, and a calculator.

During the exam

Relax! Read and think through each question and choice thoroughly, and take your time. You know the answer to that question because you've worked hard and you've been taught well. And most of all,

You got Chem ☺

Good Luck !

Table of Contents

Easy does it

. Practice a set of questions one day at a time. You'll feel less overwhelmed.

Quality over Quantity

. Complete a set, correct a set, read up on explanations, and compare your performance to previous set of the same category. You'll see your progress.

Day 1: 10 Multiple choice questions
10 points *Part A and B-1 Practice*

Start: Answer all questions on this day before stopping.

1. Which subatomic particle is negatively charged?

(1) electron
(2) neutron
(3) positron
(4) proton

2. An element that is malleable and is a good conductor of heat and electricity could have an atomic number of

(1) 16
(2) 18
(3) 29
(4) 35

3. The chemical bonding in sodium phosphate, Na_3PO_4, is classified as

(1) ionic, only
(2) metallic, only
(3) both covalent and ionic
(4) both covalent and metallic

4. At 65°C, which compound has a vapor pressure of 58 kilopascals?

(1) ethanoic acid
(2) ethanol
(3) propane
(4) water

5. Which compound is a saturated hydrocarbon?

(1) propanal
(2) propane
(3) propene
(4) propyne

6. A beta particle may be spontaneously emitted from

(1) a ground-state atom
(2) a stable nucleus
(3) an excited electron
(4) an unstable nucleus

7. The compound C_2H_4 and C_4H_8 have the same

(1) freezing point at standard temperature
(2) boiling point at standard temperature
(3) molecular formula
(4) empirical formula

8. Which particle diagram represents a mixture of elements and a compound?

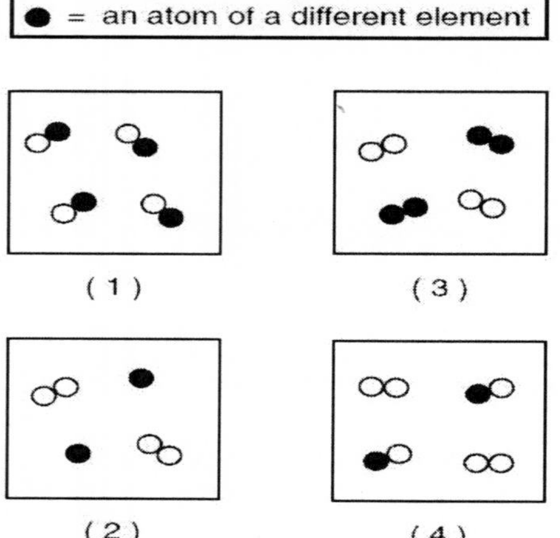

9. What is the total amount of heat absorbed by 100.0 grams of water when the temperature of the water is increased from 30.0°C to 45°C

(1) 418 J
(2) 6270 J
(3) 12 500 J
(4) 18 000 J

10. Which compound is an alkyne?

(1) C_2H_2
(2) C_2H_4
(3) C_4H_8
(4) C_4H_{10}

Day 1

Stop. Correct your answers and note how many correct **Points**

Day 1: Answers and Explanations

1. **1** *Note:* *Key phrase* in this question is "*negatively charged*"
Recall: Electrons are negatively charged particles

2. **3** *Recall:* *Malleability* and *good conductor* are physical properties of *metals*.
Relate: Element 29, Copper, is a metal

3. **3** *Note:* Sodium phosphate (Na_3PO_4) is an ionic compound with three different elements.
Recall: Ionic compounds with 3 or more elements always contain both ionic and covalent bonds

4. **2** *Recall:* Vapor pressure-temperature relationship is on Table H
Use: Reference Table H to determine answer.

5. **2** *Recall*: *Saturated hydrocarbons* are the *alkanes.*
Relate: Prop<u>ane</u> (with *–ane* name ending) is an alk<u>ane</u>.

6. **4** *Recall:* In nuclear radioactivity, ONLY *unstable nuclei spontaneously decay* by emitting a beta, an alpha or a positron particle.

7. **4** *Note:* Both C_2H_4 and C_4H_8 can be reduced (by Greatest Factor of 2) to *empirical formula* of CH_2

Day 1: Answers and Explanations

8. **4** *Recall:* An element is composed of one or more of the same atom.
A compound is composed of two or more different atoms.
Note: Diagram 4 is showing a mixture of the two.

9. **2** *Recall*: heat (q) equations are given Table T
Note: This heat question involves *temperature change.*

Choose correct heat equation, $q = mC\Delta T$ to set up and solve

Set up: $q = m \times C \times \Delta T$

Solve: $q = (100)(4.18)(15) =$ **6270 J**

10. **1** *Recall*: Table Q gives the general formula for alkynes, C_nH_{2n-2}
Determine which of the choices fits this general formula
Note: C_2H_2 is correct formula of alkyne b/c there are 2 C atoms, and the 2 H atoms is twice the # of C atoms minus 2. (2(2) – 2)

Day 2: Constructed Response Questions
10 points *Part B-2 and C Practice*

Start: Answer all questions on this day before stopping.

Base your answers to questions 1 through 3 on the information below.

Two isotopes of potassium are K-37 and K-42.

1. What is the total number of neutrons in the nucleus of a K-37 atom? [1]

2. How many valance electrons are in an atom of K-42 in the ground state? [1]

3. Explain, in terms of subatomic particles, why K-37 and K-42 are isotopes of potassium? [1]

Base your answers to questions 4 through 6 on the potential energy diagram below.

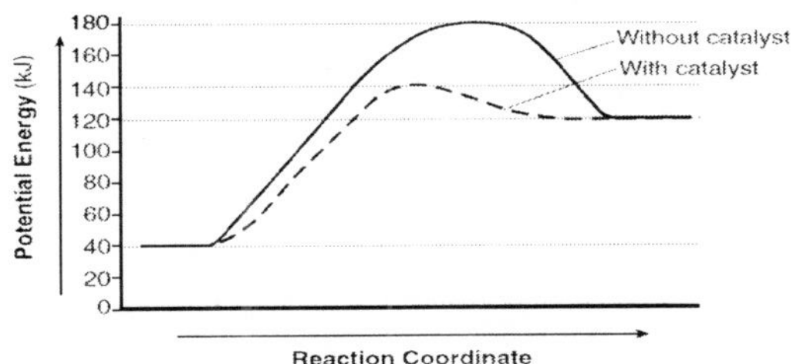

4. What is the heat of reaction for the forward reaction? [1] _____ KJ

5. What is the activation energy for the forward reaction with the catalyst? [1] ______KJ

6. Explain, in terms of the function of a catalyst, why the curves on the potential energy diagram for the catalyzed and the uncatalyzed reactions are different? [1]

Day 2: continue

Base your answers to questions 7 through 10 on the information below.

Aluminum is one of the most abundant metals in Earth's crust. The aluminum compound found in bauxite ore is Al_2O_3. Over one hundred years ago, it was difficult and expensive to isolate aluminum from bauxite ore. In 1886, a brother and sister team, Charles and Julia Hall, found that molten (melted) cryolite, Na_3AlF_6, would dissolve bauxite ore. Electrolysis of the resulting mixture caused the aluminum ions in the Al_2O_3 to be reduced to molten aluminum metal. This less expensive process is known as the Hall process.

7. Write the oxidation state for each of the elements in cryolite. [1]

8. Write a balance half-reaction equation for the reduction of Al^{3+} to Al . [1]

9. Explain, in terms of ions, why molten cryolite conducts electricity. [1]

10. Explain, in terms of electrical energy, how the operation of a voltaic cell differs from the operation of an electrolytic cell used in the Hall process. Include both voltaic cell and electrolytic cell in your answer. [1]

Day 2

Stop. Correct your answers and note how many correct **Points**

Day 2: Answers and Explanations

1. 1 point **18 neutrons**

Recall: Neutrons = Mass number - Atomic #

Calculate: Neutrons = 37 - 19 = **18**

2. 1 point **1 valance e-**

Recall: Last number in the an electron configuration is the number of valance electrons for the elements

3. 1 point Acceptable responses include, but are not limited to:

They (K-42 and K-43) have the ***same number of protons but different number of neutrons.***

4. 1 point **80 KJ**

Recall: Heat of reaction , ΔH = Hproduct – Hreactant

Determine values from graph ΔH = 120 KJ – 40 KJ

Calculate ΔH = **80 KJ**

5. 1 point **100 KJ**

Recall: Activation energy = Hactivated complex – Hreactant

Note values from graph = 140 KJ – 40 KJ

Calculate Activation energy = **100 KJ**

6. 1 point Acceptable responses include, but are not limited to:

Catalyst lowers the activation energy

Catalysts create a different or alternate pathway

Day 2: Answers and Explanations

7. 1 point **Na = + 1 Al = + 3 F = -1**

Note: You can find oxidation # of elements on the Periodic Table

Recall: The Sum of oxidation #s in a compound must equal 0

8. 1 point **Al^{3+} + 3e- -----> Al^{0}**

Recall: In Reduction, electrons lost appear Left of arrow.

Number of electrons is the difference between the two charges (+3 - 0 = 3e-)

9. 1 point Acceptable responses include, but are not limited to:

Molten (liquefied) cryolite(ionic compound) conducts electricity because it contains mobile ions.

10. 1 point Acceptable responses include, but are not limited to:

A *Voltaic cell <u>produces</u> electricity while the electrolytic cell electricity.*

Day 3: 10 Multiple choice questions
10 points *Part A and B1 Practice*

Start: Answer all questions on this day before stopping.

1. Which element has the greatest density at STP?

(1) barium
(2) beryllium
(3) magnesium
(4) radium

2. A 1.0-mole sample of krypton gas has a mass of

(1) 19 g
(2) 36 g
(3) 39 g
(4) 84 g

3. Standard pressure is equal to

(1) 1 atm
(2) 1 kPa
(3) 273 atm
(4) 273 kPa

4. According to the kinetic molecular theory, the molecules of an ideal gas

(1) have a strong attraction for each other
(2) have a significant volume
(3) move in random, constant, straight-line motion
(4) are closely packed in a regular repeating pattern

5. The isomers butane and methyl propane differ in their

(1) molecular formulas
(2) structural formula
(3) total number of atoms per molecule
(4) total number of bonds per molecule

6. In the formula X_2O , the symbol X could represent an element in Group

(1) 1
(2) 2
(3) 15
(4) 18

7. Molarity is defined as

(1) moles of solutes per kilogram of solvent
(2) moles of solute per liter of solution
(3) mass of a solution
(4) volume of solvent

Day 3: continue

8. The diagram below represents the bright-line spectra of four elements and a bright-line spectrum produced by a mixture of two of these elements.

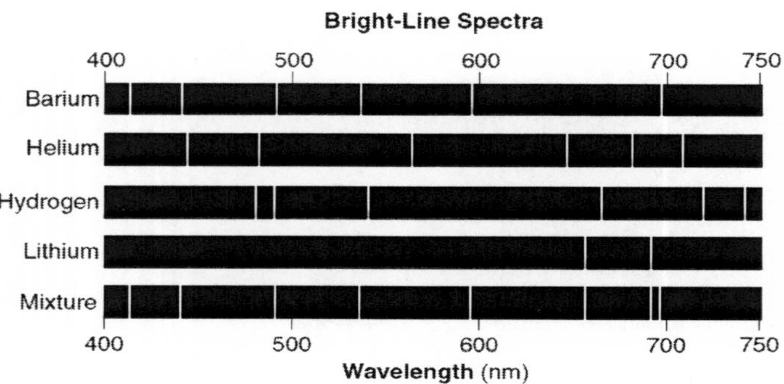

Which two elements are in this mixture?

(1) barium and hydrogen
(2) barium and lithium
(3) helium and hydrogen
(4) helium and lithium

9. Which sample, when dissolved in 1.0 liter of water, produces a solution with the lowest freezing point?

(1) 0.1 mol of C_2H_5OH
(2) 0.1 mol of LiBr
(3) 0.2 mol of $C_6H_{12}O_6$
(4) 0.2 mol of $CaCl_2$

10. Cobalt-60 and iodine-131 are radioactive isotopes that are used in

(1) dating geologic formations
(2) industrial measurements
(3) medical procedures
(4) nuclear power

Day 3

Stop. Correct your answers and note how many correct **Points**

Day 3: Answers and Explanations

1. **4** *Recall:* Density of the elements are given on Table S
Use Table S to note and compare densities of the four elements

2. **4** *Recall:* the mass of one mole of an element = Atomic mass
Note: See Periodic Table to note the Atomic mass of Kr (84 g)

3. **1** *Note:* Standard temperature and pressure are given on Table A

4. **3** *Note:* The correct answer is a fact relating the Kinetic Molecular Theory

5. **2**

Butane

```
    H   H   H   H
    |   |   |   |
H — C — C — C — C — H
    |   |   |   |
    H   H   H   H
```

methyl propane

```
    H   H   H
    |   |   |
H — C — C — C — H
    |   |   |
    H   |   H
    H — C — H
        |
        H
```

Note: Butane and methyl propane are isomers
Recall: Isomers have the same molecular formula (C_4H_{10}) but differ (are different) in their structural formulas

6. **1** *Note:* In the formula X_2O , the charge of X must be +1
Recall: If X represents a Group 1 atom (+1 charge , See Periodic Table), the oxide (oxygen compound) formula will be X_2O.

Day 3: Answers and Explanations

7. **2** *Note:* Molarity concentration equation (definition) is on Table T :

$$\text{Molarity} = \frac{\text{moles of solute}}{\text{Volume (L) of solution}}$$

8. **2** *Note:* The lines (wavelengths) in the unknown matches those given for barium and lithium

9. **4** *Recall:* Highest concentration (2.0 mol) solution will have the lowest freezing point

Recall: Ionic substances with the most ions ($CaCl_2$) will produce a solution with the lowest freezing point

10. **3** *Recall:* ***Cobalt-60*** is used in cancer treatment (a medical procedure).

Iodine-131 is used in diagnosing and treatment thyroid disorder (also a medical procedure).

Day 4: Constructed Response Questions
10 points *Part B-2 and C Practice*

Start: Answer all questions on this day before stopping.

Base your answers to questions 1 and 2 on the information below.

Archimedes (287 – 212 BC), a Greek inventor and mathematician, made several discoveries important to science today. According to a legend, Hiero, the king of Syracuse, commanded Archimedes to find out if the royal crown was made of gold, only. The king suspected that the grown consisted of a mixture of gold, tin, and copper.

Archimedes measured the mass of the crown and the total amount of water displaced by the crown when it was submerged. He repeated the procedure using individual samples, one gold, one tin, and one copper. Archimedes was unable to determine that the crown was not made entirely of gold without damaging it.

1. Identify one physical property that Archimedes used in his comparison of the metal samples. [1]

2. Determine the volume of a 75-gram sample of gold at STP. [1]

Base your answers to questions 3 and 4 on the information below.

Many esters have distinctive odors, which lead to their widespread use as artificial flavorings and fragrances. For example, methyl butanoate has an odor like pineapple and ethyl methanoate has an odor like raspberry.

3. In the space below, draw a structural formula for the ester that has an odor like pineapple. [1]

4. What is the chemical name for an alcohol that reacts with methanoic acid to produce the ester that has an odor like raspberry? [1]

Day 4: continue

Base your answers to question 5 through 7 on the information below.

A gas sample is held at constant temperature in a closed system. The volume of the gas is changed, which causes the pressure of the gas to change. Volume and pressure data are shown in the table below.

Volume and Pressure of a Gas sample

Volume (mL)	Pressure (atm)
1200	0.5
600	1.0
300	2.0
150	4.0
100	6.0

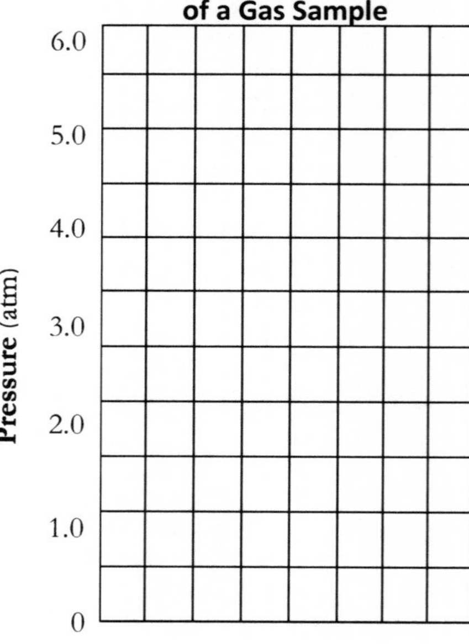

5. On the grid to the right mark an appropriate scale on the axis labeled "Volume (mL)". [1]

6. On the same grid, plot the data from the table. Circle and connect the points. [1]

   Example:

7. Based on your graph, what is the pressure of the gas when the volume o f the gas is 200. millimeters? [1] _____ atm

Day 4: continue.

Base your answers to question 8 through 10 on the information below.

A beaker contains 100.0 millimeters of a dilute aqueous solution of ethanoic acid at equilibrium. The equation below represents this system.

$HC_2H_3O_2(aq)$ < === > H+(aq) + $C_2H_3O_2$-(aq)

8. Compare the rate of the forward reaction to the rate of the reverse reaction for this system. [1]

9. Describe what happens to the concentration of H+(aq) when 10 drops of concentrated $HC_2H_3O_2(aq)$ are added to this system. [1]

10. In the space below, draw a structural formula for ethanoic acid. [1]

Day 4

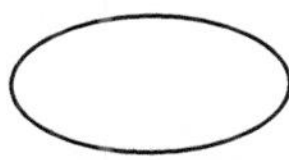

Stop. Correct your answers and note how many correct **Points**

Day 4: Answers and Explanations

1\. **1 point** **Density**

Note: Archimedes measured mass and amount of displaced water (volume)

Recall: Mass/volume) is density, which is a physical property

2\. **1 point** **3.88 cm^3**

Recall: Volume – grams relationship is Density (see Table T)

Note: Density of gold (19.3820 g/cm^3) is on Table S

Use density equation to setup and determine volume.

$$\text{Density} = \frac{\text{mass}}{\text{volume}}$$

$$\text{Volume} = \frac{75\ g}{19.3820\ g/cm^3} = \mathbf{3.88\ cm^3}$$

3\. **1 point**

```
    H   H  H  O       H
    |   |  |  ||      |
H – C – C – C – C – O – C – H
    |   |  |          |
    H   H  H          H
```

Butanoate *methyl*

4\. **1 point** **Ethanol**

5\. **1 point** ***For marking appropriate scale on the axis labeled "volume"***

6\. **1 point** ***For plotting data on the graph***

See example 2-point graph for questions 5 and 6 on the next page

Day 4: Answers and Explanations

Example two points graphing for Questions 5 and 6.

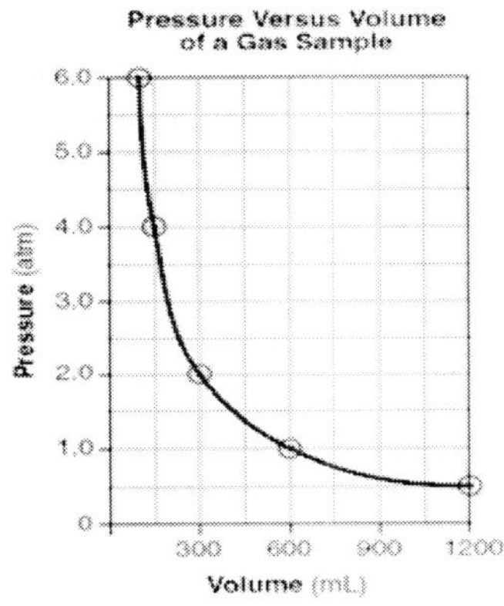

7. 1 point **3.0 atm + 0.3**

8. 1 point Acceptable responses include, but are not limited to:
The rates of forward and reverse are the equal.

Recall: This is fact about equilibrium

9. 1 point Acceptable responses include, but are not limited to:
The concentration of H+ will increase.

Recall: When concentration of a reactant increases, the concentration of products increase as well

10. 1 point

```
    H   O
    I   II
H – C – C – OH
    I
    H
```

Day 5: 10 Multiple Choice Questions
10 points *Part A and B-1 Practice*

Start: Answer all questions on this day before stopping.

1. What is the mass number of a carbon atom that contains six protons, eight neutrons, and six electrons?

(1) 6 (3) 14
(2) 8 (4) 20

2. An atom in the ground state has a stable valance electron configuration. This atom could be an atom of

(1) Al (3) Na
(2) Cl (4) Ne

3. Which equation represents an exothermic reaction at 298 K?

(1) $N_2(g)$ + $O_2(g)$ ---------> 2NO)g)
(2) C(s) + $O_2(g)$ ----------> $CO_2(g)$
(3) $KNO_3(s)$ $\xrightarrow{H_2O}$ > K+(aq)
(4) $NH_4Cl(s)$ $\xrightarrow{H_2O}$ > $NH_4^+(aq)$ + Cl-(aq)

4. Compared to the freezing and boiling point of water at 1 atmosphere, a solution of salt and water at 1 atmosphere has a

(1) lower freezing point and a higher boiling point
(2) lower freezing point and a lower boiling point
(3) higher freezing point and a lower boiling point
(4) higher freezing point and a higher boiling point

5. Which word equation represents a neutralization reaction?

(1) base + acid ----> salt + water
(2) base + salt ----> water + acid
(3) salt + acid ----> base + water
(4) salt + water ----> acid + base

6. Which particle has the greatest mass?

(1) an alpha particle (3) a neutron
(2) a beta particle (4) a positron

Day 5: continue.

7. The table below gives information about the nucleus of each of four atoms.

Atom	Number of protons	Number of neutrons
A	6	6
B	6	7
C	7	8
D	7	8

How many different elements are represented by the nuclei in the table?

(1) 1
(2) 2
(3) 3
(4) 4

8. Which process is exothermic?

(1) boiling of water
(2) melting of copper
(3) condensation of ethanol vapor
(4) sublimation of iodine

9. The chemical bond between which two atoms is most polar?

(1) C – N
(2) H – H
(3) S – Cl
(4) Si – O

10. Which nuclide has a half-life that is less than one minute?

(1) cesium-137
(2)francium-220
(3) phosphorus-32
(4) strontium-90

Day 5

Stop. Correct your answers and note how many correct **Points**

Day 5: Answers and Explanations

1. **3** *Recall:* Mass number = protons + neutrons

   14 = 6 + 8

2. **4** *Recall:* Noble gases (Group 18) have stable configurations.
   Ne is a Noble gas.

3. **2** *Recall:* Exothermic reactions have - ▲H
   Use ***Table I*** to find which reaction has a -▲H

4. **1** *Note:* The correct choice is a *fact* about property of solutions

5. **1** *Note:* The correct choice is a *fact* about neutralization reactions

6. **1** *Use* Table O to ***NOTE*** symbols of particles given as choices.
   Recall: Top number in symbols represents mass of the particle.
   $^{4}_{2}He$ (alpha) has a mass of 4, the greatest of all the particles

Day 5: Answers and Explanations

7. **2** *Recall:* Number of protons (atomic number) indicates identity of each element.

Note: The table consists of two different number of protons (6 and 7), therefore, two different elements

8. **3** *Recall:* Condensation is an exothermic (heat releasing) phase change

9. **4** *Recall*: Electronegativity Difference (ED) between two atoms in formulas can be used to determine and compare the degree of polarity of the formulas.

Recall: **Highest ED** formula is most polar, most ionic, least covalent
Lowest ED formula is Least polar, least ionic, most covalent
Use Table S to find electronegativity value for each element.

	C – N	**H – H**	**S – Cl**	**Si – O**
	N = 3.0	H = 2.1	Cl = 3.2	O = 3.5
	C = 2.6	H = 2.1	S = 2.6	Si = 1.9
ED	0.4	0	0.6	1.6
				Highest ED

10. **2** *Note:* Table N lists half-life for selected radioisotopes

Day 6: Constructed Response Questions
10 points *Part B-2 and C Practice*

Start: Answer all questions on this day before stopping.

1. Identify one ion from Table F that can combine with Pb^{2+}(aq) to produce an insoluble compound. [1]

2. Describe one appropriate laboratory test that can be used to determine the malleability of a solid sample of an element at room temperature. [1]

3. State two methods to increase the rate of a chemical reaction and explain, in terms of particle behavior, how each method increases the reaction rate. [2]

Base your answers to questions 4 through 5 on the graph below, which represents the cooling of a substance starting at a temperature above its boiling point.

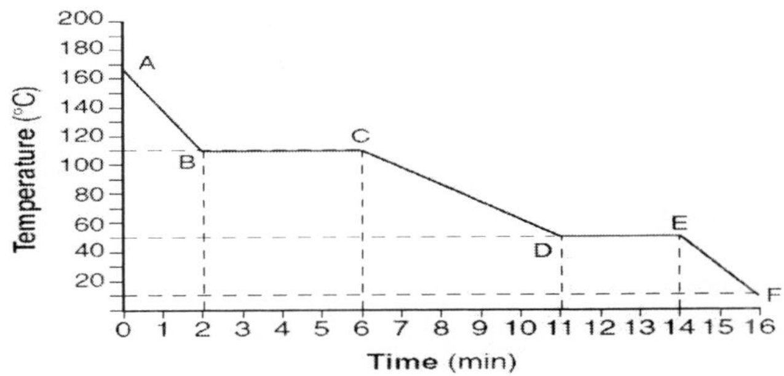

4. What is the boiling point of this substance? [1]

5. Which segment of the graph represents the gas phase, only? [1]

Day 6: continue.

Base answers to questions 6 through 9 on the information below.

Acid rain lowers the pH in pond and lakes and over time can cause the death of some aquatic life. Acid rain is caused in large part by the burning of fossil fuels in power plants and by gasoline-powered vehicles. The acids commonly associated with acid rain are sulfurous acid, sulfuric acid, and nitric acid.

In general, fish can tolerate a pH range between 5 and 9. However, even small changes in pH can significantly affect the solubility and toxicity of common pollutants. Increased concentration of these pollutants can adversely affect the behavior and normal life process of fish and cause deformity; lower egg production, and less egg hatching.

6. Acid rain caused the pH of a body of water to decrease. Explain this pH decrease in terms of the change in concentration of hydronium ions. [1]

7. Write the chemical formula of a negative polyatomic ion present in an aqueous nitric acid solution? [1]

8. Using information in the passage, describe one effect of acid rain on future generations of fish species in ponds and lakes. [1]

9. Sulfur dioxide, SO_2, is one of the gases that react with water to produce acid rain. According to Reference Table G, describe how the solubility of sulfur dioxide in water is affected by an increase in water temperature? [1]

Day 6

Stop. Correct your answers and note how many correct **Points**

Day 6: Answers and Explanations

1. **1 point** Acceptable responses include, but are not limited to:

   Cl- or **Br -** or **I-** or **F-**

   Recall: Soluble and insoluble ions are on Table F
   Note: Pb^{2+} forms insoluble ion compound with all of the halogen ions

2. **1 point** Acceptable responses include, but are not limited to:

   Hit or struck with a hammer

   Recall: ***malleability*** is defined as how easily something can be flattened into a thin sheet when struck

3. **2 point** Acceptable responses include, but are not limited to:

   Increasing temperature: ***will increase the kinetic energy of particles and allow for more frequent effective collisions.***

   Increasing pressure: ***will decrease volume and cause an increase in concentration of particles. This allows particles to collide more often.***

   Increasing surface area : ***Will expose more particles for possible collisions***

4 **1 point** **110°C**

   Note: from a graph, boiling point is the highest temperature that stayed constant for a period of time

5 **1 point** **AB**

Day 6: Answers and Explanations

6. 1 point

Acceptable responses include, but are not limited to:

A decrease in pH is caused by an increase in the hydronium ion (H_3O+) of the water.

Recall: pH value is inversely related to H_3O+ concentration. As H_3O+ concentration increases, pH decreases (becomes more acidic)

7. 1 point

NO_3^- (nitrate ion.)

Note: Nitric acid formula is HNO_3 (see Table K)
Note: Polyatomic ions are listed on Table E

8. 1 point

Acceptable responses include, but are not limited to:

There'll be a smaller population of the fish species.

There'll be greater number of fish with abnormality.

9. 1 point

Acceptable responses include, but are not limited to:

Solubility of SO_2 decreases as water temperature increases

As water temperature increases, so does the solubility of SO_2

Day 7: 10 Multiple Choice Questions
10 points *Part A and B-1 Practice*

Start: Answer all questions on this day before stopping.

1. Which conclusion was a direct result of the gold foil experiment?
   (1) An atom is mostly empty space with a dense positively charged nucleus
   (2) An atom is composed of at least three types of subatomic particles
   (3) An electron has a positive charge and is located inside the nucleus
   (4) An electron has properties of both waves and particles

2. Which atom has an atom with the greatest attraction in a chemical bond?
   (1) As
   (2) Bi
   (3) N
   (4) P

3. Which formula represents a polar molecule?
   (1) Br_2
   (2) CO_2
   (3) CH_4
   (4) NH_3

4. In which sample is the average kinetic energy of particles greatest?
   (1) 10. mL of HCl(aq) at 25°C
   (2) 15. mL of HCl(aq) at 20°C
   (3) 10. mL of H_2O(l) at 35°C
   (4) 15. mL of H_2O(l) at 30°C

5. System in nature tend to undergo changes toward
   (1) lower energy and less disorder
   (2) lower energy and more disorder
   (3) higher energy and less disorder
   (4) higher energy and more disorder

6. Which half-reaction equation represents the reduction of a potassium ion?
   (1) K^+ + e- ----> K
   (2) K + e- -----> K^+
   (3) K^+ ---> K + e-
   (4) K ----> K+ + e-

Day 7: continue.

7. Which two notations represent different isotopes of the same element?

(1) $^{6}_{4}Be$ and $^{9}_{4}Be$

(2) $^{7}_{3}Li$ and $^{7}_{3}Li$

(3) $^{14}_{7}N$ and $^{14}_{6}C$

(4) $^{32}_{15}P$ and $^{32}_{16}S$

8. Reduction occurs at the cathode in

(1) electrolytic cells, only
(2) voltaic cells, only
(3) both electrolytic cells and voltaic cells
(4) neither electrolytic cells nor voltaic cells

9.The table below shows data for the the temperature, pressure, and volume of four gas samples.

Gas samples	Temperature (K)	Pressure (atm)	Volume (mL)
A	100.	2	400.
B	200.	2	200.
C	100.	2	400
D	200.	4	200

Which two gas samples have the same total number of molecules?

(1) A and B
(2) A and C
(3) B and C
(4) B and D

10. What is the gram-formula mass of $Ca_3(PO_4)_2$?

(1) 248 g/mol
(2) 263 g/mol
(3) 279 g/mol
(4) 310. g/mol

Day 7

Stop. Correct your answers and note how many correct **Points**

Day 7: Answers and Explanations

1. **1** *Note:* Correct choice is *facts* about gold foil experiment

2. **3** *Recall:* Electronegativity measures atom's ability to attract e-.
   Note: Table S gives electronegativity values for the elements.
   Recall: The higher the electronegativity value of an element, the more likely it will attract electrons.
   Note: N has the highest electronegativity value of those given.

3. **4** *Recall:* *Polar* molecules have *asymmetrical* structures.
   Note: The rest of the choices will have symmetrical structures.
   Recall: NH_3 has an asymmetrical structure.

```
H – N – H
    |
    H
```

4. **3** *Recall:* Temperature is a measure of average kinetic energy
   The higher the temperature, the greater the average kinetic energy of its particles.
   Note: 35°C is the highest temperature given as a choice

5. **2** *Note*: the correct choice is a *fact* about chemical & physical systems

6. **1** *Recall:* In reduction, electrons gained appear to the left of arrow.
   Note: The sum of charges must be equal on both sides

Day 7: Answers and Explanations

7. **1** *Note:* isotope symbols must have the same bottom number (that matches the atomic number of the element) but different top numbers (different mass numbers)

8. **3** *Note:* This a fact of similarity between voltaic and electrolytic

Recall: REDuction occurs at CAThode (REDCAT) in both cells.

9. **2** *Recall*: Avogadro's law states that "equal volume of gases at the same temperature and pressure contain equal number of molecules"

10. **4** *Recall:* formula mass is the sum of all atomic masses in a formula

Break up formula : $Ca_3(PO_4)_2$ 3 Ca 2 P 8 O

Setup: *Multiply* by (atomic mass) 3(40) + 2(31) + 8 (16)

Add up products: 120 + 62 + 128 = **310 g**

Note: Values in ( ) are the rounded atomic mass located on the Periodic Table for the elements.

Day 8: Constructed Response Questions
10 points Part B-2 and C Practice

Start: Answer all questions on this day before stopping.

Base your answers to questions 1 and 2 on the information below.

A light bulb contains argon gas at a temperature of 295 K and a pressure of 75 kilopascals. The light bulb is switch on, and after 30 minutes its temperature is 418 K. Assume the volume of the light bulb remains constant.

1. In the space below show a correct numerical setup for calculating the pressure of the gas inside the light bulb at 418 K. Assume the volume of the light bulb remains constant. [1]

2. What Celsius temperature is equal to 418 K ? [1] ___^{o}C

Base your answers to questions 3 through 5 on the diagram of a voltaic cell and the balance ionic equation below.

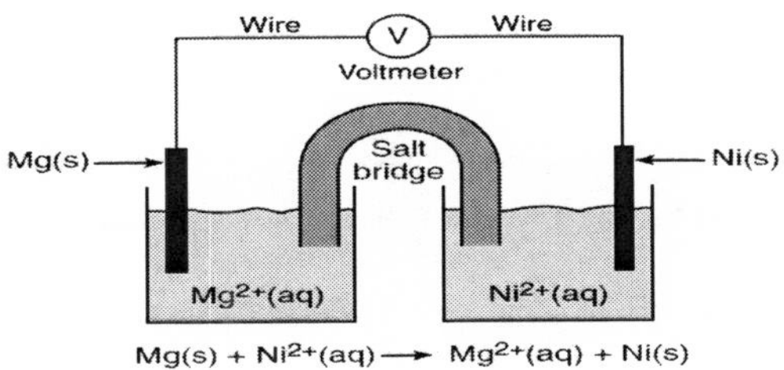

3. What is the total number of moles of electrons needed to completely reduce 6.0 moles of Ni^{2+}(aq) ions? [1] ____ mol

4. Identify one metal from Reference Table J that is more easily reduced than Mg(s) . [1]

5. Explain the function of salt bridge in the voltaic cell. [1]

Day 8: continue

Base your answers to questions 6 and 7 on the information below.

The unbalanced equation below represents the decomposition of potassium chlorate.

$KClO_3(s)$ ---- > $KCl(s)$ + O_2

6. Balance the equation below using the smallest whole-number coefficients. [1]

____$KClO_3(s)$ ---- > ____ $KCl(s)$ + ___ O_2 (g)

7. Determine the oxidation number of chlorine in the reactant. [1]

Base your answers to questions 8 through 10 on the information below.

In living organisms, the ratio of the naturally occurring isotopes of carbon, C-12 and C-13 to C-14, is fairly consistent. When an organism such as a wooly mammoth died, it stopped taking in carbon, and the amount of C-14 present in the mammoth began to decrease. For example, one fossil of a woolly mammoth is found to have $^{1}/_{32}$ of the amount of C-14 found in a living organism.

8. Identify the type of nuclear reaction that caused the amount of C-14 in the woolly mammoth to decrease after the organism died. [1]

9. Determine the total time that has elapsed since this woolly mammoth died. [1]

______ y

10. State, in terms of subatomic particles, how an atom of C-13 is different from an atom of C-12. [1]

Day 8

Stop. Correct your answers and note how many correct **Points**

Day 8: Answers and Explanations

1\. 1 point

$$\frac{75}{295} = \frac{X}{418} \quad \text{or} \quad \frac{(75)(418)}{295}$$

Note: This is a gas law problem that is setup with the combined gas law equation on Table T :

$$\frac{P_1}{T_1} = \frac{P_2}{T_2}$$

Note from question and passage:

P_1 = 75 kPa P_2 = unknown X

T_1 = 295 K T_2 = 418 K

Volume (V) remains constant, so it is eliminated from the combined gas law equation

2\. 1 point

145°C

Recall: equation for converting temperature is on Table T

Setup using equation   K = °C + 273

Solve   418 = **145 °C** + 273

3\. 1 point

12 moles of e-

Note: This many electrons is required to equalized charges when **6 moles** of Ni^{2+} is reduced.

The equations below offer clearer explanations

From question   **1** Ni^{2+} + **2**e- ------> **1** Ni

Proportion equation   **6** Ni^{2+} + ***12*** e- ------> **6** Ni

4\. 1 point

Acceptable response includes, but are not limited to:

Any metal below *Mg* ***(Al to Au)*** is acceptable answer

Recall: On Table J, a metals is more easily reduced than another element if it is below that element.

5 1 point

Acceptable response includes, but are not limited to:

Salt bridge provides a path of movement (migration) of ions.

Note: this answer is just a definition of a salt bridge

Day 8: Answers and Explanations

6. 1 point **2** $KClO_3$ -----> **2** KCl + **3** O_2

7. 1 point **+5**

Recall: sum of charges in a compound must equal zero (0)

Note: In $KClO_3$ K = +1 1(+1) = +1 (total + so far)

O = -2 3(-2) = -6 total – in formula

Determine charge of Cl : Must be **+5** for charges to equal 0

8. 1 point Acceptable response includes, but are limited to :

Alpha decay

Natural transmutation

Note: Decay mode (alpha) for C-14 is listed on Table N
Recall: Alpha decay is a type of natural transmutation

9. 1 point **28650 y**

Recall: Fraction Remaining equation is on Table T
Use fraction $^1/_{32}$ to determine # of half-life periods (n)

Fraction Remaining = $^1/_{32}$ = $^1/_{2n}$ n = 5

Use equation below to determine length of time
Length of Time = half-life x n
= 5730 x 5 = **28650 y**

Note: Half-life of C-14 (5730 yrs) is given on Table N

10. 1 point Acceptable response includes but are limited to:
C-13 has a different number (more) neutrons than C-12

Note: C-12 and C-13 are isotopes

Recall: isotopes are different because of the different numbers of neutron

Day 9: 10 Multiple Choice Questions
10 points *Part A and B-1 Practice*

Start: Answer all questions on this day before stopping.

1. In the wave-mechanical model of the atom, orbitals are regions of the most probable locations of

(1) protons
(2) positrons
(3) neutrons
(4) electrons

2. As the elements of Group 17 are considered in order of increasing atomic number, there is an increase in

(1) atomic radius
(2) electronegativity
(3) first ionization energy
(4) number of electrons in the first shell

3. What is the chemical formula for iron (III) oxide?

(1) FeO
(2) Fe_2O_3
(3) Fe_3O
(4) Fe_3O_2

4. Given a formula for oxygen:

$$\ddot{\underset{..}{O}} = \ddot{\underset{..}{O}}$$

What is the total number of electrons shared between the atoms represented in this formula?

(1) 1
(2) 2
(3) 8
(4) 4

5. What is the IUPAC name of the organic compound that has the formula shown below?

```
                H
                |
              H-C-H
                |
      H  H  H   |   H
      |  |  |   |   |
    H-C- C- C - C - C-H
      |  |  |   |   |
      H  H  H   H   H
```

(1) 1,1-dimethylbutane
(2) 2-methylpentane
(3) hexane
(4) 4-methylpentane

Day 9: continue.

6. Given the balance equation representing a reaction:

$$Mg(s) + Ni^{2+}(aq) \text{ -------> } Mg^{2+}(aq) + Ni(s)$$

What is the total number of moles of electrons lost by Mg(s) when 2.0 moles of electrons are gained by $Ni^{2+}(aq)$?

(1) 1.0 mol
(2) 2.0 mol
(3) 3.0 mol
(4) 4.0 mol

7. When 5 grams of KCl are dissolved in 50. grams of water at 25°C, the resulting mixture can be described as

(1) heterogeneous and unsaturated
(2) heterogeneous and supersaturated
(3) homogeneous and unsaturated
(4) homogeneous and supersaturated

8. Starting as a solid, a sample of a substance is heated at a constant rate. The graph below shows the changes in temperature of this sample.

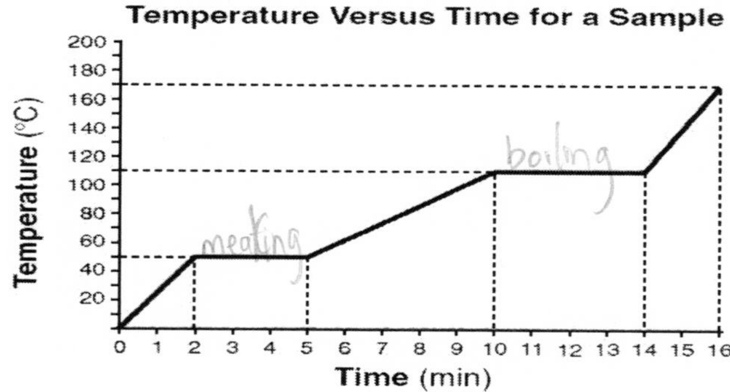

What is the melting point of the sample and the total time required to completely melt the sample after it has reached its melting point?

(1) 50°C and 3 min
(2) 50°C and 5 min
(3) 110°C and 4 min
(4) 110°C and 14 min

Day 9: continue.

9. A sample of a gas occupies a volume of 50. millimeters in a cylinder with a movable piston. The pressure of the sample is 0.90 atmospheres and the temperature is 298 K. What is the volume of the sample at STP?

(1) 41 mL
(2) 49 mL
(3) 51 mL
(4) 55 mL

10. Which general formula represents the compound CH_3CH_2CCH?

(1) C_nH_n
(2) C_nH_{2n}
(3) C_nH_{2n-2}
(4) C_nH_{2n+2}

Day 9

Stop. Correct your answers and note how many correct **Points**

Tracking your progress

If you have completed Day 1, 3, 5, 7 and 9 multiple choice question sets, you can easily check your progress and improvements in this question category.

. Go to page 211

. Plot and graph the number of points you got correct on each of the days using the first graph on the page (the 10-point graph)

You hope to see an upward trend on the graph, which will indicates improvement and progress.

If you are not satisfied with your performance and progress, we recommend that you study a bit from your review packets and books before continuing to next sets of questions in this book.

Day 9: Answers and Explanations

1. **4** *Note:* The correct choice is a facts relating to orbitals

2. **1** *Note*: Atomic radius refers to the size of atoms.
Recall trend: From top to bottom (increase atomic number), each successive atom has one more electron shell (therefore larger) than an atom before it.

3. **2** *Note:* a formula is correct when it has correct symbols of atoms (or ions) and correct number (subscript) of each atom.
Recall: When writing formulas for Iron (III) oxide
Use Periodic Table to get symbols and charges Fe^{3+} O^{2-}
Use criss-cross method to get correct subscripts Fe_2O_3
Note: (III) indicates a charge of 3+ for iron (Fe)

4. **4** *Recall:* Each single bond (–) in a formula represents two shared e-
Relate: In O = O , the double bond (=) represents 4 shared e-

5. **2** *Note:* The correct name reflects these facts about the structure.
The methyl is on the second C atom (from left): 2-methyl
There are 5 C atoms (pent) in the long single bonded (alkane) chain. pentane

6. **2** *Note:* The mole ratio in the balanced redox equation is 1 : 1
Relate: **2** moles of e- gained by Ni^{2+} = **2** moles of e- lost by Mg

Day 9: Answers and Explanations

7. **3** *Note:* Part of the answer to this question requires using Table G.

According to Table G

In 100 g H_2O at 25°C: 35.0 g of KCl forms a saturated solution

In 50 g H_2O at 25°C : 17.5 g of KCl will be a saturated solution

(Half the amount of H_2O) (Half the grams of KCl)

Note: only ***5 g*** of KCl is in solution in the question

Recall: a solution (which is always a homogeneous mixture) containing less (5g KCl) than the saturated amount (17.5 g) is ***unsaturated***

8. **1** *Note* From the graph: melting occurs between the 2nd and 5th minutes (*a total of 3 minutes*) at *50°C*

9. **1** *Note*: This is a Gas law problem:

Use Combined Gas Law equation on Table T to setup and solve for the new volume

$$\frac{P_1V_1}{T_1} = \frac{P_2V_2}{T_2}$$

$$\frac{(.9)(50)}{298} = \frac{1(X)}{273} \qquad \textit{Setup}$$

298 X = (.9) (50) (273 *Cross-multiply to get*

X = 41.2 mL *Calculated result for V_2*

10. **3** *Note* the following about the formula: CH_3CH_2CCH (C_4H_6)

there are 4 C 6 H (the number of H is twice the number of C minus 2)

Relate: This formula fits the general formula C_nH_{2n-2} (Listed on Table Q for alkynes)

Day 10: Constructed Response Questions

10 points ***Part B-2 and C Practice***

Start: Answer all questions on this day before stopping.

1. What is the oxidation number of nitrogen in NO(g) ? [1]

   2

2. Write an electron configuration for an atom of aluminum-27 in an excited state. [1]

   2-7-4

3. What color is bromcresol green after it is added to a sample of NaOH(aq)? [1]

   Blue

4. Because tap water is highly acidic, water pipes made of iron erode over time, as shown by the balanced ionic equation below:

   $$2Fe + 6H^+ \text{------>} 2Fe^{3+} + 3H_2$$

   Explain, in terms of chemical reactivity, why copper pipes are less likely to corrode than iron pipes. [1]

   because Cu is less reactive than Fe

Base your answers to questions 5through 6 on the information below.

Given the balance equation for an organic reaction between butane and chlorine that takes place at 300°C and 101.3 kilopascals:

$$C_4H_{10} + Cl_2 \text{----->} C_4H_9Cl + HCl$$

5. Identify the type of organic reaction shown. [1]

   Substitution reaction

6. In the space below, draw the structural formula for the organic product. [1]

   H H H H
   H-C-C-C-C-Cl
   H H H H

7. Explain, in terms of collision theory, why the rate of the reaction would decrease if the temperature of the reaction mixture was lowered to 200.°C with pressure remaining unchanged. [1]

   Collision will drop due to the decrease to the kinetic energy

Day 10: continue.

Base your answers to questions 7 through 9 on the data in Reference Table S.

8. On the data table below record the boiling points for He, Ne, Ar, Kr, and Xe. [1]

9. On the grid below, plot the boiling points of He, Ne, Ar, Kr, and Xe. Circle and connect the points. [1]

Example:

Data Table

Symbol	Atomic Number	Boiling Point (K)
He	2	4
Ne	10	27
Ar	18	87
Kr	36	121
Xe	54	166

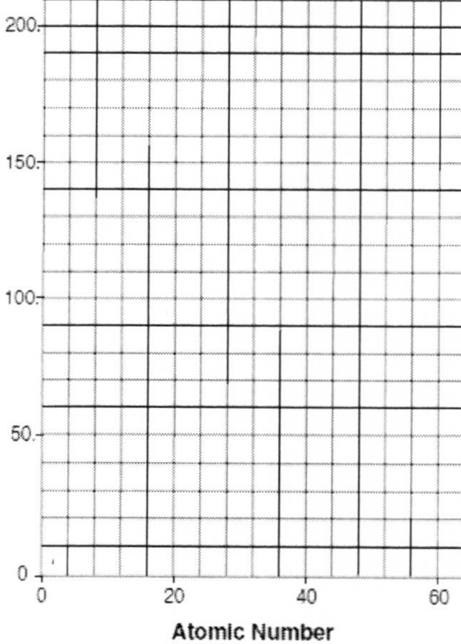

10. Base on your graph, describe the trend in the boiling points of these elements as the atomic number increases. [1]

As the atomic number increase, the boiling point increase

Day 10

Stop. Correct your answers and note how many correct **Points**

Day 10: Answers and Explanations

1. 1 point **+2**

Recall: sum of charges must equal 0 in compounds

Note: in NO O has a charge of -2 (See Periodic Table)

Determine charge of N: N must be +2 for charges to equal

2. 1 point Acceptable responses include, but are not limited to:

2 – 8 – 2 – 1 **2 – 7 – 4** **1 – 8 – 4**

Note: The excited state configurations must still have 13 e-

3. 1 point **Blue** will be the color of bromcresol green when added to NaOH.

Note: NaOH is a base with pH greater then 7.

According to Table M, bromcresol green will change from yellow to blue at a pH range of 3.8 – 5.4. That means any solution with a pH greater than 3.8 will be blue.

4. 1 point Acceptable responses include, but are limited to:

Copper, Cu, is less reactive than Fe .

Iron, Fe, is more reactive than copper

Note: On Table J, the element that is higher up(Fe) is always more reactive than an element that is lower down (Cu).

5. 1 point **Substitution reaction.**

Note: In equation, the organic reactant is C_4H_{10} (an alkane)

The organic product is C_4H_9Cl (a halide) with one halogen

Recall: Substitution reactions involve an alkane reactant and halide product

6. 1 point

```
    H   H   H   H
    |   |   |   |
H – C – C – C – C – Cl
    |   |   |   |
    H   H   H   H
```

Note : Your structure may variation:

The Cl can be bonded to any of the C atoms.

Day 10: Answers and Explanations

7. 1 point Acceptable Response includes, but are limited to:
Rate of the reaction will decrease when temperature is decreased **particles will collide less frequently due to a decrease in their average kinetic energy.**

8. 1 point **For completing the column labeled "Boiling Point (K)" with values highlighted below**

Data Table

Symbol	Atomic Number	Boiling Point (K)
He	2	4
Ne	10	27
Ar	18	87
Kr	36	121
Xe	54	166

9. 1 point **For plotting the points and graphing.**

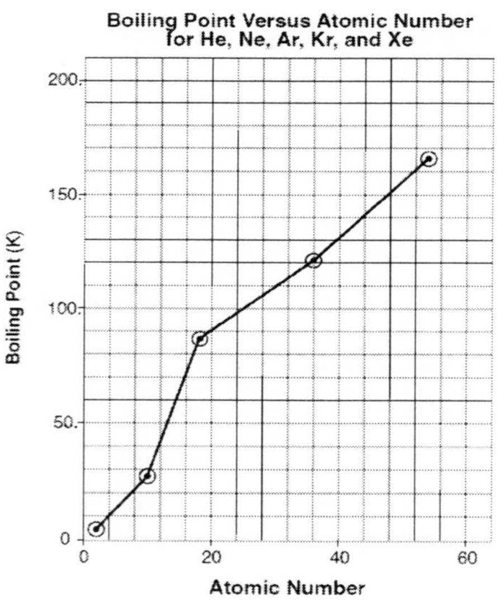

Example of 1-point graph for 9

10. 1 point Acceptable response includes, but are not limited to:
As atomic number increases, boiling point increases.
Note: Your answer may vary based on your graph

Day 11: 15 Multiple Choice Questions

15 points ***Part A and B-1 Practice***

Start: Answer all questions on this day before stopping.

1. Which particle has a mass approximately the same as the mass of a proton?

   (1) an alpha particle
   (2) a beta particle
   (3) a neutron
   (4) a positron

2. The most common isotope of chromium has a mass of 52. Which notation represents a different isotope of chromium?

   (1) $^{52}_{24}Cr$
   (2) $^{54}_{24}Cr$
   (3) $^{24}_{52}Cr$
   (4) $^{24}_{54}Cr$

3. Which substance can be broken down by chemical means?

   (1) CO
   (2) Ce
   (3) Ca
   (4) Cu

4. The bonds in BaO are best described as

   (1) covalent, because valance electrons are shared
   (2) covalent, because valance electrons are transferred
   (3) ionic, because valance electrons are shared
   (4) ionic, because valance electrons are transferred

5. The net energy released or absorbed during a reversible chemical reaction is equal to

   (1) the activation energy of the endothermic reaction
   (2) the activation energy of the exothermic reaction
   (3) the difference in the potential energy of products and the potential energy of the reactants
   (4) The sum of the potential energy of the products and the potential energy of the reactants

6. Which class of organic compounds has a molecule that contain nitrogen atom?

   (1) alcohol
   (2) amine
   (3) ether
   (4) ketone

Day 11: continue.

7. Which particle is emitted when an atom of ^{85}Kr spontaneously decay?

(1) an alpha particle
(2) a beta particle
(3) a neutron
(4) a proton

8. Which equation represents a physical change?

(1) $H_2O(s)$ + 6.0 KJ -----> $H_2O(l)$
(2) $2H_2(g)$ + $O_2(g)$ -------> $2H_2O(g)$ + 483.6 KJ
(3) $H_2(g)$ + $I_2(g)$ + 53.0 KJ -------> 2HI(g)
(4) N2(g) + $2O_2(g)$ + 66.4 KJ ----> $2NO_2(g)$

9. Magnesium and calcium have similar chemical properties because an atom of each element has the same number of

(1) electron shells
(2) valance electrons
(3) neutrons
(4) protons

10. An iron bar at 325 K is placed in a sample of water. The iron bar gains energy from the water if the temperature of the water is

(1) 65 K
(2) 45 K
(3) 65°C
(4) 45°C

11. Given the equation representing a reaction at equilibrium.

$NH_3(g)$ + $H_2O(l)$ <====> $NH_4^{+(}aq)$ + OH- (aq

The H+ acceptor for the forward reaction is

(1) $H_2O(l)$
(2) $NH_3(g)$
(3) $NH^{4+(}aq)$
(4) OH-(aq)

Day 11: continue.

12. The diagram below represents the nucleus of an atom.

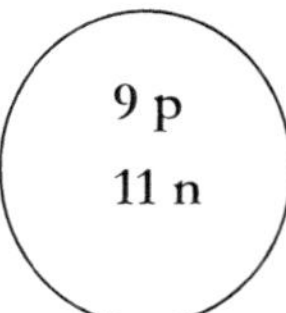

What are the atomic number and the mass number of this atom?

(1) The atomic number is 9 and the mass number is 19
(2) The atomic number is 9 and the mass number is 20
(3) The atomic number is 11 and the mass number is 19
(4) The atomic number is 11 and the mass number is 20

13. Which list of elements consists of metalloids?

(1) B, Al, Ga
(2) C, N, P
(3) O, S, Se
(4) Si, Ge, As

14. Which volume of 0.10 M NaOH(aq) exactly neutralizes 15.0 millimeters of 0.20 M HNO_3 (aq) ?

(1) 1.5 mL
(2) 7.5 mL
(3) 3.0 mL
(4) 30. mL

15. Which fraction of an original 20.00-gram sample of nitrogen-16 remains unchanged after 36.0 seconds?

(1) $^1/_5$
(2) $^1/_8$
(3) $^1/_{16}$
(4) $^1/_{32}$

Day 11

Stop. Correct your answers and note how many correct **Points**

Day 11: Answers and Explanations

1. **3** *Recall:* Both protons and neutrons have mass of 1 amu

2. **2** *Note:* Isotope symbol for Chromium– 52 is $^{52}_{24}Cr$ (52 ← mass #; 24 ← atomic #)

   Recall: A different isotope of an element (Cr) must have a different top number (**mass #**) and the same bottom number (***atomic #)*** $^{54}_{24}Cr$

3. **1** *Recall:* Compounds can be broken down.

   Note: CO is a compound b/c it is composed of two different elements.

4. **4** *Note:* BaO is composed of a metal (Ba) and a Nonmetal (O)

   Recall: Ionic bond is formed by transfer of electrons between a metal atom and a nonmetal atom.

5. **3** *Note:* Net energy (heat absorbed or released) is Heat of reaction (ΔH)

   Recall: ΔH = Hproduct - Hreactant
   (difference between energy of product and that of reactant)

6. **2** *Recall:* Classes of organic compounds are on Reference Table R

7. **2** *Recall:* Particles emitted by selected radioisotope are on Table N

8. **1** *Note:* The correct equation is showing a phase change, which is a a type of physical change

9. **2** *Note:* Both Mg and Ca are in Group 2

   Recall: Elements in the same Group react in similar manners due to them having same number of valance electrons.

Day 11: Answers and Explanations.

10. **3** *Recall:* heat flows from high to low temperature

Note: for heat to be gained by the iron (at 325 K) from water, the water must have a temperature higher than 325 K.

Determine: 65°C (338 K) is higher than 325 K.

NOTE: to covert Celsius to Kelvin use: K = °C + 273 (Table T)

11. **2** *Note:* according to the equation, NH_3 accepts a H+ to become NH_4^+

NH_3 + H_2O -------> NH_4^+ + OH-

H^+ (proton) acceptor — *H^+(proton) donor*

12. **2** *Recall:* Atomic number (9) = number of protons (9p)

Recall: Mass number (20) = Protons (9) + neutrons (11)

13. **4** *Use* Periodic Table to note elements that are metalloids

14. **4** *Note:* This is a titration problem

Use titration equation on Table T to setup and solve for volume

$$M_A V_A = M_B V_B$$

Setup (0.20)(15.0) = (0.10) (X)

Solve 30 mL = X

Day 11: Answers and Explanations.

15. **4** *Note:* This is a half-life problem that can be solved in two steps.

First: Calculate number of half-life periods (n) from times.

$$n = \frac{\text{length of time (T)}}{\text{half- life (t)}} = \frac{36}{7.2} = 5$$

Note: half-life of N-16 (7.2 sec) is on Table N

Second: Calculate Fraction remaining using Table T equation

$$\text{Fraction remaining} = \frac{1}{2^n} = \frac{1}{2 \times 2 \times 2 \times 2 \times 2} = \mathbf{\frac{1}{32}}$$

Day 12: Constructed Response Questions
10 points *Part B-2 and C Practice*

Start: Answer all questions on this day before stopping.

Base your answers to questions 1 through 3 on the information below.

The particle diagrams below represent the reaction between two nonmetals, A_2 and Q_2.

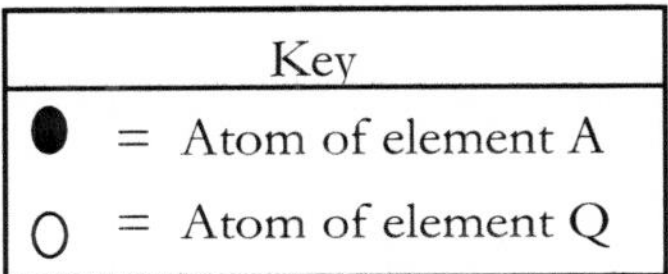

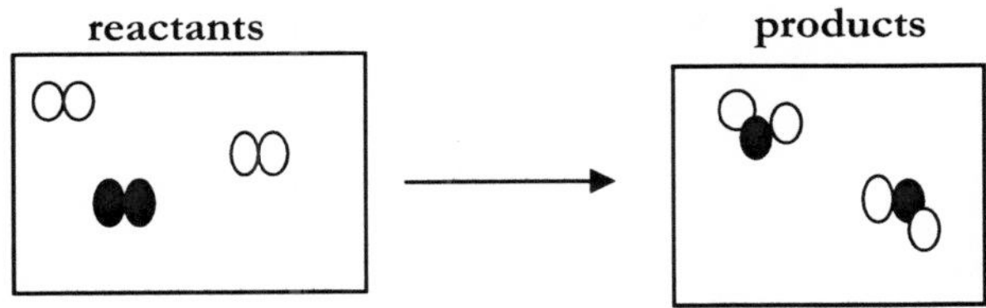

1. Using the symbols A and Q, write the chemical formula of the product. [1]

2. Identify the type of chemical bond between an atom of element A and an atom of element Q. [1]

3. Compare the total mass of the reactants to the total mass of the product. [1]

Day 12: continue.

4. In the space below, calculate the formula mass of glucose, $C_6H_{12}O_6$. Your answer must include the correct numerical setup and the calculated result. [2]

show setup [1]

_________ g/mol
calculated result [1]

5. What is the empirical formula for the compound $C_6H_{12}O_6$. [1]

Base your answers to questions 6 through 9 on the information below.

In the laboratory, a glass tube is filled with hydrogen gas at a very low pressure. When a scientist applies a high voltage between metal electrodes in the the tube, light is emitted. The scientist analyzes the light with a spectroscope and observes four distinct spectral lines. The table below gives the color, frequency, and energy from each of the four spectral lines. The unit for frequency is hertz, Hz.

Visible Spectrum of Hydrogen

Color	Frequency ($\times 10^{14}$ Hz)	Energy ($\times 10^{-19}$ J)
Red	4.6	3.0
Blue green	6.2	4.1
Blue	6.9	4.6
Violet	7.3	4.8

6. On the grid below, plot the data from the data table for frequency and energy. Circle and connect the points, including the point (0,0) that has already been plotted and circled for you. [1]

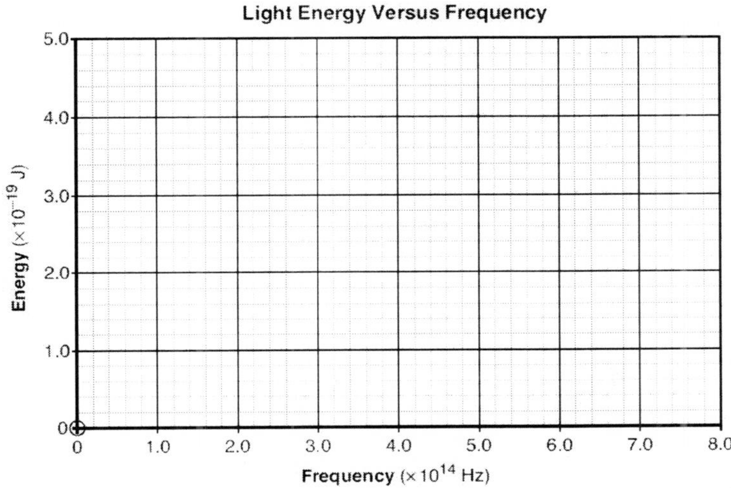

7. A spectral line in the infrared region of the spectrum of hydrogen has a frequency of 2.3×10^{14} hertz. Using your graph, estimate the energy associated with this spectral line. [1]

__________ $\times 10^{-19}$

8. Explain, in terms of subatomic particles and energy states, why light is emitted by the hydrogen gas. [1]

9. Identify one condition not mentioned in the passage, under which hydrogen gas behaves most like an ideal gas. [1]

Day 12

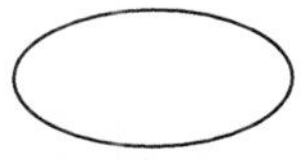

Stop. Correct your answers and note how many correct **Points**

Day 12: Answers and Explanations

1. 1 point ***AQ*** $_2$

Note: The product is composed of 1A and 2 Q's

2. 1 point ***Polar Covalent*** *or* ***covalent***

Note: Both A and Q are nonmetals (according to the passage).

Recall: Bonding between two nonmetals is covalent

3. 1 point ***They are the same or equal***

Note: Number of atoms of reactants and products are the same

Recall: In chemical reactions, mass (as well as charges, energy, and atoms) are always conserved

4. 2 points ***180*** *g*

In $C_6H_{12}O_6$ there are

6 C 12 H 6 O

6 (12) + 12(1) + 6(16) ← Set-up (**1 point**). May vary

72 + 12 + 96 = ***180 g*** ← calculated result (**1 point**)

Note: Allow point for formula mass that is consistent with your setup

5. 1 point ***CH_2O***

Recall: To get empirical formula, reduce subscripts of

molecular formula , $C_6H_{12}O_6$, by the Greatest Common Factor (6)

Day 12: Answers and Explanations

6. 1 point **For plotting and connecting the dots.**

Example of a 1-point graph for number 6.

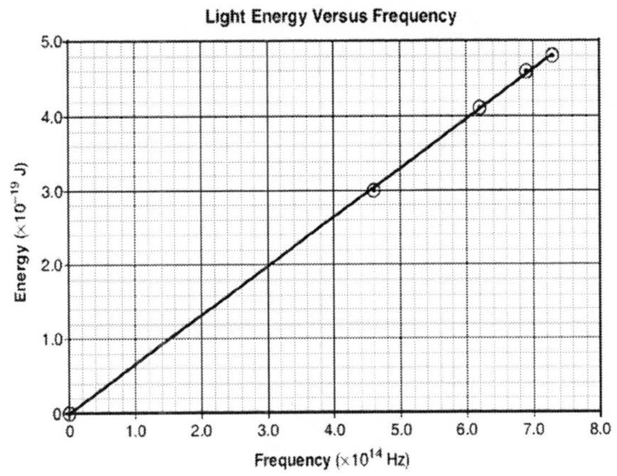

7. 1 point **1.5** $\times 10^{-19}$ J $\pm$ **0.1** $\times 10^{-19}$ J

Allow point for a value that is consistent with your graph.

8. 1 point Acceptable responses include, but are not limited to:

Light is emitted by hydrogen when:

electrons return from excited state to the ground state.

electrons go from high to low energy level

9. 1 point Acceptable responses include, but are not limited to:

Hydrogen gas will behave most like an ideal gas under:

Low pressure
High temperature.

Track your progress

If you have completed Day 2, 4, 6, 8, 10, and 12 constructed response question sets, then you are half-way through with sets of questions in this category. You can easily check your progress and improvements in this question category.

. Go to page 212

. Plot and graph the number of points you got correct on each of these days

You hope to see an upward trend on the graph, which indicates improvement and progress.

If you are not satisfied with what your performance and progress, we recommend that you study a bit from your review packets or books before continuing with to the next sets of constructed response questions in this book.

Day 13: 15 Multiple Choice Questions

15 points ***Part A and B-1 Practice***

Start: Answer all questions on this day before stopping.

1. Which quantity identifies an element?

(1) atomic number
(2) mass number
(3) total number of neutrons in an atom of the element
(4) total number of valance electrons in an atom of the element

2. Which element has the greatest density?

(1) calcium
(2) carbon
(3) chlorine
(4) copper

3. Which equation shows conservation of atoms?

(1) H_2 + O_2 -----> H_2O
(2) H_2 + O_2 ------> $2H_2O$
(3) $2H_2$ + O_2 ----> $2H_2O$
(4) $2H_2$ + $2O_2$ ----> $2H_2O$

4. A solid substance is an excellent conductor of electricity. The chemical bonds in this substance are mostly

(1) ionic, because valance electrons are shared between atoms
(2) ionic, because the valance electrons are mobile
(3) metallic, because the valance electrons are stationary
(4) metallic, because the valance electrons are mobile

5. Which barium salt is insoluble in water?

(1) $BaCO_3$
(2) $BaCl_2$
(3) $Ba(ClO_4)_2$
(4) $Ba(NO_3)_2$

6. Which substance is an Arrhenius acid?

(1) $Ba(OH)_2$
(2) CH_3COOCH_3
(3) H_3PO_4
(4) NaCl

7. Which energy conversion occurs in a voltaic cell?

(1) chemical energy to electrical energy
(2) chemical energy to nuclear energy
(3) electrical energy to chemical energy
(4) nuclear energy to electrical energy

8. Which reaction converts an atom of one element to an atom of another element?

(1) combustion
(2) polymerization
(3) saponification
(4) transmutation

9. Which two samples of gas at STP contain the same total number of molecules?

(1) 1 L of $CO(g)$ and 0.5 mol of $N_2(g)$
(2) 2 L of $CO(g)$ and 0.5 L of $NH_3(g)$
(3) 1 L of $H_2(g)$ and 2 L of $Cl_2(g)$
(4) 2 L of $H_2(g)$ and 2 L of $Cl_2(g)$

10. Which element is a brittle solid with low conductivity?

(1) sulfur
(2) sodium
(3) argon
(4) aluminum

11. Which change in pH represents a hundred fold increase in the concentration of hydronium ions in a solution?

(1) pH 1 to pH 2
(2) pH 1 to pH 3
(3) pH 2 to pH 1
(4) pH 3 to pH 1

12. What is the empirical formula for a compound with the molecular formula of $C_6H_{12}Cl_2O_2$?

(1) CHClO
(2) CH_2ClO
(3) C_3H_6ClO
(4) $C_6H_{12}Cl_2O_2$

13. Which compound is a member of the same homologous series as C_3H_8?

(1) CH_4
(2) C_4H_8
(3) C_5H_8
(4) C_5H_{10}

Day 13: continue.

14. The potential energy diagram for a chemical reaction is shown below.

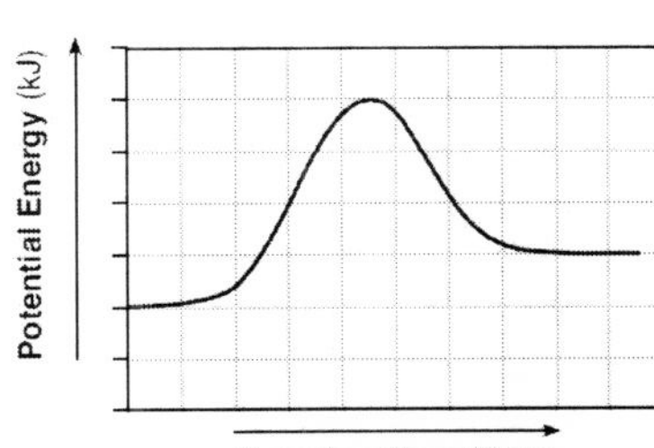

Each interval on the axis labeled "Potential Energy (KJ)" represents 40 kilojoules. What is the heat of reaction?

(1) -120 KJ
(2) -40 KJ
(3) +40 KJ
(4) +160 KJ

15. Given the balanced equation representing a nuclear reaction:

$$^{235}_{92}U + ^{1}_{0}n \text{ -----> } ^{142}_{56}Ba + ^{91}_{36}Kr + 3X + \text{energy}$$

Which particle is represented by X?

(1) $^{0}_{-1}e$
(2) $^{1}_{1}H$
(3) $^{4}_{2}He$
(4) $^{1}_{0}n$ 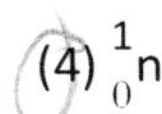

Day 13

Stop. Correct your answers and note how many correct **Points**

Day 13: Answers and Explanations

1. **1** *Recall:* Each element has its own unique atomic number

2. **4** *Use* Table S to note and compare densities of the elements

3. **3** *Recall:* only balanced equations show conservation of atoms (as well as mass, charges and energy)
   Note: The correct equation is balanced because there are equal number of atoms (4 H and 2 O) on each side.

4. **4** *Recall:* Only Metallic substances conduct electricity in the solid phase (due to their mobile valance electrons)

5. **1** *Use* Table F to determine soluble and insoluble compounds
   Note: According to Table F, CO_3^{2-} (carbonate) ions form insoluble salts (even with Ba).
   In all other choices, the ions form soluble salt with Ba .

6. **3** *Use* Table K to determine formulas of Arrhenius acids
   Note: H_3PO_4 is listed on Table K

7. **1** *Note:* Correct choice is a fact of energy change in voltaic cells

8. **4** *Note:* Key phrase in question *"convert one atom to another atom"*.
   Recall: Transmutation is defined as a conversion of one atom to another

9. **4** *Recall:* Avogadro's law states equal volume of gases at same condition contains sane number of molecules
   Note: The two gases in choice 4 are the same volume

Day 13: Answers and Explanations

10. **1** *Recall:* Brittleness and low conductivity describe nonmetallic solids.
Relate: Sulfur is a nonmetal.

11. **4** *Recall:* A decrease in pH (becomes more acidic) is a result of an increase in hydronium (H_3O^+) or hydrogen ion (H+) concentration .

Recall: 10 fold increase in H_3O^+ = 1 value decrease in pH
100 fold increase in H_3O^+ = 2 values decrease in pH
Correct choice (pH 3 to pH 1) is a 2 value decrease

12. **3** *Determine* Greatest Common Factor and reduce subscripts by that factor.
Note: $C_6H_{12}Cl_2O_2$ has GCF of 2, and can be reduced to C_3H_2ClO

13. **1** *Note:* C_3H_8 fits general formula for alkanes,C_nH_{2n+6} (See Table Q)
Note: CH_4 is also an alkane, therefore, same homologous series

14. **3** *Note* from diagram: Hproduct (120 KJ) and Hreactant (80 KJ).
Recall: Heat of reaction (ΔH) = **Hproduct** – Hreactant
Calculate: Heat of reaction (ΔH) = 120 KJ – 80 KJ = **+40 KJ**

15. **4** *Note:* The equation represent fission reaction
Recall: neutrons ($^{1}_{0}n$) are also released during fission process.

Day 14: Constructed Response Questions
10 points ***Part B-2 and C Practice***

Start: Answer all questions on this day before stopping.

Base your answers to questions 1 though 3 on the data table below.

Formulas and Boiling Points of Selected Alkanes.

Name	Formulas	Boiling Point at 1 ATM (°C)
methane	CH_4	-162
ethane	C_2H_6	-89
propane	C_3H_8	-42
butane	C_4H_{10}	-0.5
pentane	C_5H_{12}	36

1. In the space below, draw a structural formula for butane. [1]

2. At standard pressure and 298 K, which alkane is a liquid? [1]

3. What is the boiling point of propane at 1 atmosphere, in Kelvins? [1]

Day 14: continue.

Base your answers to questions 4 through 6 on the information below.

A piece of magnesium ribbon is reacted with excess hydrochloric acid to produce aqueous magnesium chloride and hydrogen gas. The volume of the dry hydrogen gas produced is 45.6 millimeters. The temperature of the gas is 283 K, and the pressure is 99.5 kilopascals.

4. Balance the equation below using the smallest whole-number coefficients. [1]

1 Mg(s) + 2 HCl(aq) ---> 1 $MgCl_2$(aq) + 1 H_2(g)

5. Identify the type of bond between atoms in a molecule of the gas produced in this laboratory investigation. [1]

Covalent

6. Calculate the volume this dry hydrogen gas would occupy at STP. [1]

_____ mL

Base your answers to questions 7 and 8 on the information below.

A solution is made by completely dissolving 90. grams KNO_3(s) in 100. grams of water in a beaker. The temperature of this solution is 65°C.

7. Describe the effect on the solubility of KNO_3(s) in this solution when the pressure on the solution increases. [1]

No change in Solubility

8. Determine the total mass of KNO_3(s) that settles to the bottom of the beaker when the original solution is cooled to 15°C. [1]

90g - 30g = 60g

Day 14: continue.

Base your answers to questions 9 and 10 on the information below.

A 4.86 gram sample of calcium reacted completely with oxygen to form 6.80 grams of calcium oxide. This reaction is represented by the balanced equation below.

$2\,Ca(s) + O_2(g) \text{ -----> } 2CaO(s)$

9. Determine the total mass of oxygen that reacted. [1]

4.86g + 1.94 = 6.80

10. Explain, in terms of electrons, why the radius of a calcium ion is smaller than the radius of a calcium atom. [1]

Ca^{2+} has fewer eletrons

Day 14

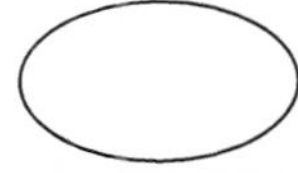

Stop. Correct your answers and note how many correct **Points**

Day 14: Answers and Explanations

1. 1 point

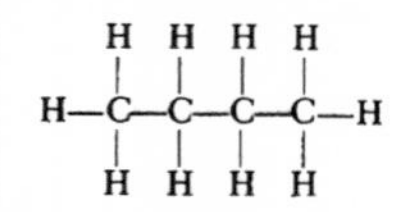

butane, C_4H_{10}

Recall: Butane is a four C atom alkane (single bond between C atoms, and 10 H atoms)

2. 1 point

Pentane

Note: it has the highest boiling point, therefore, will be a liquid.

3. **1 point**

231 K

Use equation K = °C + 273 (Table T)

231 = -41 + 273

4. 1 point

_Mg + **<u>2</u>** HCl -----> _$MgCl_2$ + _H_2

5. 1 point

Acceptable response include, but are not limited to :

Nonpolar covalent

Covalent

Note: H_2 (H – H) gas is produced.

Recall: Bonding between two of the same nonmetal (H) atoms is always nonpolar covalent

Day 14: Answers and Explanations

6. 1 point **43.2 millimeter**

Note: This is a gas law problem

Determine factors from *passage* and *question:*

$V_1 = 45.6$ mL $T_1 = 283$ K $P_1 = 99.5$ kPa *from passage*

$V_2 = X$ $T_2 = 273$ K $P_2 = 101.3$ kPa *from question*

STP (see Table A)

Use the Combined Gas Law to set up and solve

$$\frac{P_1 V_1}{T_1} = \frac{P_2 V_2}{T_2}$$

$$V_2 = \frac{P_1 V_1 T_2}{T_1 P_2}$$

$$V_2 = \frac{(99.5)(45.6)(273)}{(283)(101.3)} = \mathbf{43.2\ ml}$$

7. 1 point Acceptable responses include, but are not limited to:

No change in solubility

Solubility stays the same

Recall: Pressure change has no effect on solubility of a solid such as $KNO_3(s)$

8. 1 point **60 grams**

Use Table G: saturation amount of KNO_3 at 15°C = 30g

Calculate the amount that settle to bottom (did not dissolve)

Grams KNO_3 in solution – saturated grams at 15°C

90 g – 30 g = **60g**

Day 14: Answers and Explanations

9. 1 point **1.94 g**

Recall: According to Law of Conservation of matter:

Total Mass of Reactants = Total Mass of Products

Ca	+	O_2	------ >	$2\ CaO$
4.86 g	+	**1.94 g**	=	6.80 g

10. 1 point Acceptable responses include, but are not limited to:

Radius of a calcium ion (Ca^{2+}) is smaller than the radius of a calcium atom (Ca) because

A calcium ion has 2 fewer electrons than a calcium atom

Ca^{2+} has 1 fewer electron shell than a Ca atom

Note: Ca forms a Ca^{2+} ion (See Periodic Table).

Recall: an atom becomes a positive ion by losing electrons

Day 15: 15 Multiple Choice Questions
15 points ***Part A and B-1 Practice***

Start: Answer all questions on this day before stopping.

1. Which statement describes the relative energy of the electrons in the shell of a calcium atom?
   (1) An electron in the first shell has more energy than an electron in the second shell
   (2) An electron in the first shell has the same amount of energy as an electron in the second shell
   (3) An electron in the third shell has more energy than an electron in the second shell
   (4) An electron in the third shell has less energy than an electron in the second shell

2. Which Group 14 element is a metalloid?
   (1) tin
   (2) silicon
   (3) lead
   (4) carbon

3. Which formula represents a molecular compound?
   (1) Kr
   (2) LiOH
   (3) N_2O_4
   (4) NaI

4. A reaction is most likely to occur when reactant particle collide with
   (1) proper energy, only
   (2) proper orientation, only
   (3) both proper energy and proper orientation
   (4) neither proper energy nor proper orientation

5. Which element is present in every organic compound?
   (1) carbon
   (2) fluorine
   (3) nitrogen
   (4) oxygen

6. What is the total number of valance electrons in an atom of germanium in the ground state?
   (1) 8
   (2) 2
   (3) 14
   (4) 4

Day 15: continue.

7. A 50.0-gram block of copper at 10.°C is carefully lowered into 100.grams of water at 90°C in insulated container. Which statement describes the transfer of heat in this system?

   (1) The water loses heat to the block until both are at 90.0°C.
   (2) The block gains heat from the water until both are at 90.0°C.
   (3) The water loses heat and the block gains heat until both are at the same temperature that is between 10.0°C and 90.0°C.
   (4) The water gains heat and the block loses heat until both are at the same temperature that is between 10.0°C and 90.0°C.

8. Given the reaction below;

$$CH_3C(=O)-OH + HOC_2H_5 \rightleftharpoons CH_3C(=O)-O-C_2H_5 + H_2O$$

   This reaction is an example of

   (1) fermentation
   (2) saponification
   (3) hydrogenation
   (4) esterification

9. Which balanced equation represents a redox reaction?

   (1) PCl_5 ----> PCl_3 + Cl_2
   (2) KOH + HCl ------> KCl + H_2O
   (3) LiBr -----> Li+ + Br-
   (4) Ca^{2+} + SO_4^{2-} ----> $CaSO_4$

10. What is the total number of protons in an atom with the electron configuration of 2 – 8 – 18 – 32 – 18 – 1 ?

   (1) 69
   (2) 79
   (3) 118
   (4) 197

11. Which compound contains both ionic and covalent bond?

   (1) ammonia
   (2) sodium nitrate
   (3) methane
   (4) potassium chloride

Day 15: continue.

12. What is the percent composition by mass of hydrogen in NH_4HCO_3 (gram-formula mass = 79 grams per mole)

(1) 5.1 %
(2) 6.3 %
(3) 10. %
(4) 50. %

13. Which particle model diagram represents only one compound composed of elements X and Z?

Key
● = atom of X
○ = atom of Z

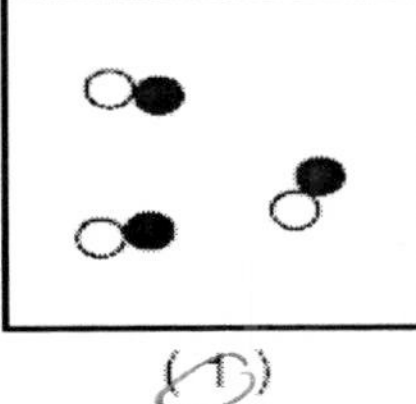
(1)

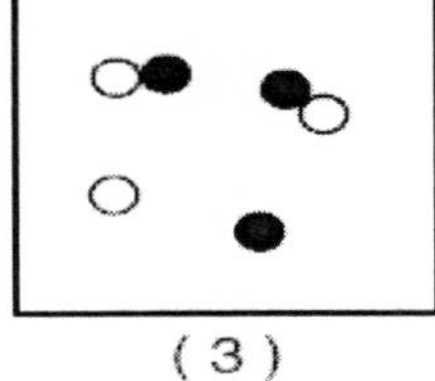
(3)

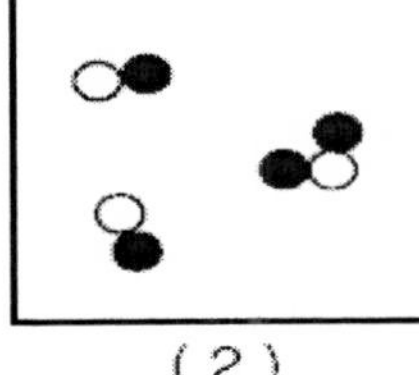
(2)

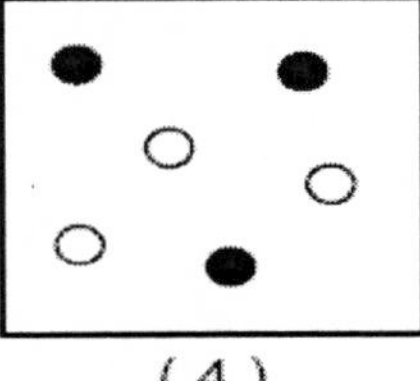
(4)

Day 15: continue.

14. Which 1-mole sample has the least entropy?

(1) $Br_2(s)$ at 266 K
(2) $Br_2(l)$ at 266 K
(3) $Br_2(l)$ at 332 K
(4) $Br_2(g)$ at 332 K

15. An original sample of K-40 has a mass of 25.00 grams. After 3.9×10^9 years, 3.125 grams of the original remains unchanged. What is the half-life of K-40?

(1) 1.3×10^9 y
(2) 2.6×10^9 y
(3) 3.9×10^9 y
(4) 1.2×10^{10} y

Day 15

Stop. Correct your answers and note how many correct **Points**

Day 15: Answers and Explanations

1. **3** *Recall:* an electron absorbed energy to move to a higher shell
   Relate: an electron at a higher shell (3rd) always has more energy than an electron at a lower shell (2nd)

2. **2** *Locate* each of the elements on the Periodic Table.

3. **3** *Recall:* Chemical formulas of molecular compounds contains two or more different nonmetal atoms (N and O).

4. **3** *Note:* The answer is a fact related to collision theory

5. **1** *Note*: The answer is a fact about organic (carbon-based) compounds

6. **4** *Note:* Configuration of Ge on the Periodic Table is 2–8– 8–4
   Recall: Last number (4) is always the # of valance electrons

7. **3** *Recall:* Heat flows (or is lost) from higher temp to lower temp.
   Relate: Higher temp (water) will lose heat to the lower temp (cu)
   Note: equilibrium temperature must always be between that of the two temps.

8. **4** *Use* Table R to determine classes of organic compounds given in the equation.

$$\underset{\text{organic acid}}{CH_3C(=O)-OH} + \underset{\text{alcohol}}{HOC_2H_5} \rightleftharpoons \underset{\text{ester}}{CH_3C(=O)-O-C_2H_5} + \underset{\text{water}}{H_2O}$$

Recall: Esterification reactions involve an organic acid and alcohol

or

Note: The main product is an ester.
Relate: The reaction is esterification b/c an ester is produced.

Day 15: Answers and Explanations

9. **1** *Recall:* single replacement, decomposition and synthesis reactions are all considered redox reactions.

Note: Choice 1 equation is a synthesis reactions.

or

Recall: a reaction equation is a redox if there is a change of oxidation numbers (lost and gained of electrons)

Note: Both P and Cl go through changes in oxidation numbers

10. **2** *Recall :* number of electron = number of protons (Atomic #)

Note: numbers in configuration are number of electrons

Sum of numbers in the configuration

2 – 8 – 18 – 32 – 18 – 1 = 79 = number of protons

11. **2** *Recall:* compounds containing both ionic and covalent bonds likely contain a polyatomic ion or have three or more elements

Note: Sodium nitrate ($NaNO_3$) contains a polyatomic ion (NO_3). It also contains three different elements

12. **2** *Note:* Percent composition equation is on Table T

$$\% H = \frac{\text{total mass of } 5\text{ H}}{\text{formula mass}} \times 100$$

$$\% H = \frac{5}{79} \times 100 = \mathbf{6.3\ \%}$$

13. **1** *Recall:* A diagram of a compound must show the two different atoms touching (bonding)

All units in the diagram must be identical.

Note: Only the diagram for choice 1 that these are the case

Day 15: Answers and Explanations

14. **1** *Recall:* Entropy describes disorder (chaos, randomness) of particles.

In terms of :

Temperature: Least entropy must be at lowest temp. (266 K)

Phase: Lowest entropy must be a solid. $Br_2(s)$

15. **1** *Note:* This is a half-life problem that can be solved in two steps.

First: Determine number of half-life period (n) from masses.

25 g ---> 12.5 ----> 6.25 ----> 3.125 g

(3 arrows = 3 half-life periods, n)

Second: Use equation below to determine the half-life

$$\textbf{Half-life} = \frac{\text{Length of time}}{\text{Half-life periods (n)}} = \frac{3.9 \times 10^9}{3} = \mathbf{1.3 \times 10^9\ y}$$

Day 16: Constructed Response Questions
10 points *Part B-2 and C Practice*

Start: Answer all questions on this day before stopping.

Base your answers to questions 1 through 3 on the information below.

A 100.0-gram sample of NaCl(s) has an initial temperature of 0°C. A chemist measures the temperature of the sample as it is heated. Heat is not added at a constant rate. The heating curve for the sample is shown below.

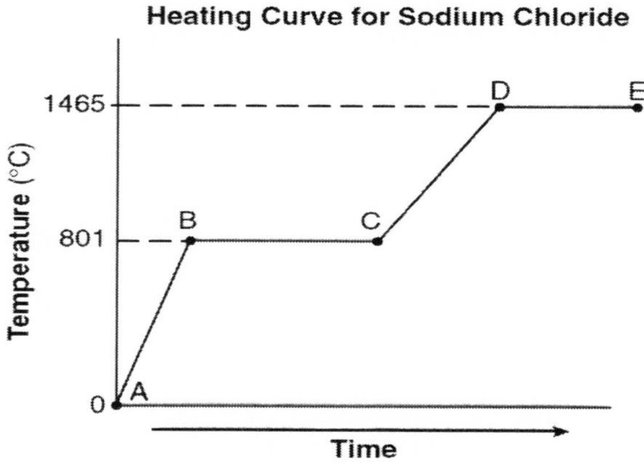

1. Determine the temperature range over which the entire NaCl sample is a liquid. [1]

2. Identify one line segment on the curve where the average kinetic energy of the particles of the NaCl sample is changing. [1]

3. Identify one line segment on the curve where the NaCl sample is in a single phase and capable of conducting electricity. [1]

Day 16: continue.

Base your answers to questions 4 through 6 on the information below.

Elements with atomic number 112 and 114 have been produced and their IUPAC names are pending approval. However, an element that would be put between these two on the Periodic Table has not yet been produced. If produced, this element will be identify by the symbol Uut until an IUPAC name is approved.

4. In the space below, draw Lewis electron-dot diagram for an atom of Uut. [1]

uut

5. Determine the charge of an Uut nucleus. Your response must include both the numerical value and the sign of the charge. [1]

+133

6. Identify one element that would be chemically similar to Uut. [1]

 Al

Day 16: continue.

Base your answers to questions 7 through 10 on the information below.

When a person perspires (sweats), the body loses many sodium ions and potassium ions. The evaporation of sweat cools the skin. After a strenuous workout, people often quench their thirst with sport drinks that contain NaCl and KCl. A single 250.0 grams serving of one sport drink contains 0.055 gram of sodium ions.

7. In the space below, show a numerical setup for calculating the concentration of sodium ions in this sport drinks, expressed as percent by mass. [1]

8. Describe the transfer of energy between skin and the surroundings as a person perspires and the sweat evaporates. [1]

Heat is lost by the skin and gained by the Surrounding

9. State why the salts in sport drinks are classified as electrolytes. [1]

Salt in sports drinks allowed for electrical

10. In the space in your answer booklet, draw a Lewis electron-dot diagram for one of the positive ions lost by the body as a person perspires. [1]

Na^+

Day 16

Stop. Correct your answers and note how many correct **Points**

Day 16: Answers and Explanations

1. 1 point **CD**

Recall where different phases are represented on a phase change diagram.

2. 1 point **AB** or **CD**

Recall: average kinetic energy only changes when there is a change in temperature.

Note: Based on the diagram, temperature of the substance is changing during segments AB and CD

3. 1 point **CD**

Recall: ionic solids (such as NaCl) can only conduct electricity in the liquid (or aqueous) phase.

Relate: Segment CD represents the liquid phase of the substance

4. 1 point **:Uut.**

Note: Uut will have atomic number of 113 (a number between 112 and 114) according to the passage.

Based on this atomic number, Uut will be in Group 13

Note: Since all Group 13 elements have 3 valance electrons, the Lewis electron –dot diagram will have 3 dots around the symbol Uut

5. 1 point **+113**

Recall: nuclear charge (+) = atomic number (113)

6. 1 point **B, Al, Ga, In,** or **Ti**

Recall: Elements in the same Group are chemically similar.

Relate: any Group 13 element is chemically similar to Uut

Day 16: Answers and Explanations

7. 1 point

$$\frac{.055\ g}{250\ g} \times 100 \quad \text{or} \quad \frac{5.5}{250\ g}$$

Note: $\% \text{ of Na ion} = \dfrac{\text{mass of Na ion}}{\text{total mass of sport drink}} \times 100$

8. 1 point

Acceptable responses include, but are not limited to:

Heat is lost by the skin and gained by the surrounding
Heat will flow from the skin to the surrounding

9. 1 point

Acceptable responses include, but are not limited to:

mobile ions of the salt in sports drinks allow for electrical conductivity.

Recall: Electrolytes are substances that can conduct electricity in solution

10. 1 point

Na^+ or **K^+**

Note: the two + ions are Na^+ and K^+

Recall: Lewis electron-dot diagrams for a +ions is just the symbol of the ion

Day 17: 15 Multiple Choice Questions
15 points *Part A and B-1 Practice*

Start: Answer all questions on this day before stopping.

1. An atom of an element forms a 2+ ion. In which Group on the Periodic Table could this element be located?

   (1) 1
   (2) 2
   (3) 13
   (4) 17

2. During all chemical reactions, mass, energy, and charge are

   (1) absorbed
   (2) conserved
   (3) formed
   (4) released

3. Samples of four Group 15 elements, antimony, arsenic, bismuth, and phosphorus, are in the gaseous phase. An atom in the ground state of which element requires the least amount of energy to remove its most loosely held electron?

   (1) As
   (2) Bi
   (3) P
   (4) Sb

4. An atom of an element has a total of 12 electrons. An ion of the same element has a a total of 10 electrons. Which statement describes the charge and radius of the ion?

   (1) The ion is positively charged and its radius is smaller than the radius of the atom
   (2) The ion is positively charged and its radius is larger than the radius of the atom
   (3) The ion is negatively charged and its radius is smaller than the radius of the atom
   (4) The ion is negatively charged and its radius is larger than the radius of the atom

5. At STP, which 2.0 gram sample of matter uniformly fills a 340-millimeters closed container?

   (1) $Br_2(l)$
   (2) $Fe(NO_3)_2(s)$
   (3) KCl(aq
   (4) Xe(g)

6. At standard pressure, which element has a freezing point *below* standard temperature?

   (1) In
   (2) Ir
   (3) Hf
   (4) Hg

Day 17: continue.

7. Changes in activation energy during chemical reaction are presented by a

(1) cooling curve
(2) heating curve
(3) ionization energy diagram
(4) potential energy diagram

8. An aqueous solution of lithium hydroxide contains hydroxide ions as the only negative ion in the solution. Lithium hydroxide is classified as an

(1) aldehyde
(2) alcohol
(3) Arrhenius acid
(4) Arrhenius base

9. Given the balanced equation representing a reaction:

$$4Al(s) \quad + 3O_2(g) \quad \text{----->} \quad 2Al_2O_3(s)$$

Which type of chemical reaction is represented by this equation?

(1) double replacement
(2) single replacement
(3) substitution
(4) synthesis

10. What is the total mass of a solute in 1000. grams of a solution having a concentration of 5 parts per million?

(1) 0.005 g
(2) 0.05 g
(3) 0.5 g
(4) 5 g

11. Which indicator would best distinguish between a solution with a pH of 3.5 and a solution with a pH of 5.5?

(1) bromthymol blue
(2) bromcresol green
(3) litmus
(4) thymol blue

12. Which half-reaction correctly represents reduction?

(1) Mn^{4+} -----> Mn^{3+} + e-
(2) Mn^{4+} -----> Mn^{7+} + 3e-
(3) Mn^{4+} + e- ------> Mn^{3+}
(4) Mn^{4+} + 3e- ------> Mn^{7+}

Day 17: continue.

13. The table below indicates the stability of six nuclides.

Stability of Six Nuclide

Nuclide	Stability
C-12	stable
C-14	unstable
N-14	stable
N-16	unstable
O-16	stable
O-19	unstable

All atoms of the unstable nuclide listed in this table have

(1) an odd number of neutrons
(2) an odd number of protons
(3) more neutrons than protons
(4) more protons than neutrons

14. What is the oxidation number of sulfur in $Na_2S_2O_3$?

(1) -1
(2) +2
(3) +6
(4) +4

15. Which two compounds have the same molecular formula but different chemical and physical properties?

(1) CH_3CH_2Cl and CH_3CH_2Br
(2) CH_3CHCH_2 and $CH_3CH_2CH_3$
(3) CH_3CHO and CH_3COOCH_3
(4) CH_3CH_2OH and CH_3OCH_3

Day 17

Stop. Correct your answers and note how many correct **Points**

Day 17: Answers and Explanations

1. **2** *Look* on the Periodic Table for charges listed for Group 2

2. **2** *Note:* The correct choice is a fact about Law of conservation

3. **2** *Recall:* Ionization energy values (Table S) indicate energy needed to remove most loosely bound e- of an atom
Use Table S to note and compare ionization energy values.
Note: Of all the choices, Bi has the lowest energy

4. **1** *Note:* an ion with 2 less electrons than the atom has +2 charge.
Recall: The size of a + ion is always smaller than that of the atom

5. **4** *Recall:* Gases have no definite volume, so they take (fill) the space of their containers
Relate: Xe(g) is a gas.

6. **4** *Recall:* Standard temperature is 273 K. (See Table A)
Note: Use Reference Table S to get and compare the freezing points (same as melting points) of the elements
Note: Hg has a melting point (freezing point) of of 234 K, which is lower than standard temperature of 273 K.

7. **4** *Recall:* Potential energy diagram shows energy changes of substances during a reaction.

8. **4** *Note:* hydroxides (as in lithium hydroxide) are names of bases.
Recall: names and formulas of bases are on Table L

9. **4** *Note:* The equation shows two elements (Al and O_2) combining to make one substance Al_2O_3
Recall: Synthesis reactions involve two or more substances combining to make one substance

Day 17: Answers and Explanations

10. **1** *Note:* This is parts per million concentration problem
Use parts per million equation (Table T) to setup and solve

$$\text{ppm} = \frac{\text{Grams of solute}}{\text{Grams of solution}} \times 1\,000\,000$$

Grams of solute = $\frac{\text{ppm} \times \text{grams of solution}}{1\,000\,000}$

Grams of solute = $\frac{5 \times 1000}{1\,000\,000}$ = **0.005 g**

11. **2** *Note:* An indicator (Table M) is good for distinguishing between two solutions of different pH if the indicator will change different colors in the two solution.

Note: According to pH range for bromcresol green (Table M)
In a solution with pH 3.5, bromcresol green will be yellow.
In a solution with pH 5.5, bromcresol green will be blue.

12. **3** *Recall:* a correct reduction equation must show :
electrons (e-) lost to the left of arrow
and
sum of charges must be equal on both sides

Note: Mn^{4+} + e- ----> Mn^{3+} is a correct reduction equation because e- is left of arrow and sum of charges are equal (+3) on both sides.

13. **3** *Note:* This choice is the only true information for all the unstable nuclei: They each have more ***neutrons*** (mass # - atomic #) than **protons** (atomic #)

Note: unstable nuclei	mass # =	**protons (atomic #)** +	***neutrons***
C-14	14	**6**	***8***
N-16	16	**7**	***9***
O-19	19	**8**	***11***

Day 17: Answers and Explanations

14. **2** *Recall:* sum of all charges in a formula must equal zero

Note: In $Na_2S_2O_3$

Na	=	+1	=	2 (+1)	=	+2	(total positive so far)
O	=	-2	=	3 (-2)	=	-6	(total negative)
Charge of S	=	+2	=	2 (+2)	=	+4	(additional positive)
						0	**net charge**

Note: Total + charge needed from S so charges can be equal to 0 is +4.
However, there are 2 S atoms in the formula.
Therefore, each S must be a **+2 charge**

15. **4** *Recall:* isomers are organic compounds with the same molecular formula (same number of atoms) but different chemical structures (different properties)

Note: This choice is correct because the number of C, H and O atoms are the same in both formulas.

CH_3CH_2OH	and	CH_3OCH_3	(choice 4)
2 C	=	2 C	
6 H	=	6 H	
1 O	=	1 O	

Day 18: Constructed Response Questions

10 points ***Part B-2 and C Practice***

Start: Answer all questions on this day before stopping.

1. Describe one chemical property of Group 1 metals that results from the atoms of each metal having only one valance electrons. [1]

   Gourp 1 metals bond with most elements.

2. Given the balance equation representing a reaction:

   $N_2(g) + O_2(g) + 182.6\ KJ \dashrightarrow 2NO(g)$

   On the labeled axes below, draw a potential energy diagram for this reaction . [1]

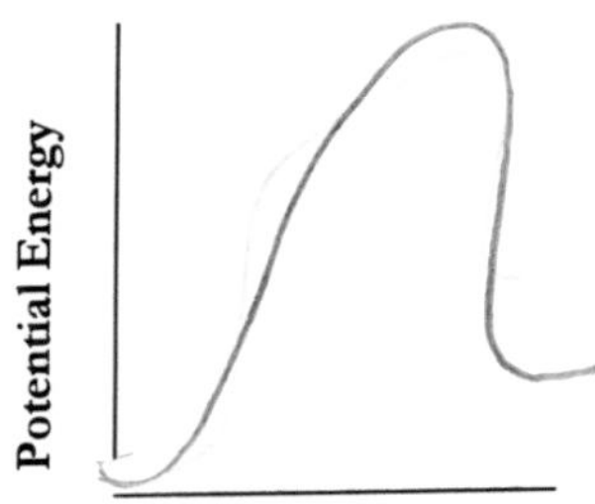

Reaction Coordinate

melting
solid
liq
gas

3. Write one electron configuration for an atom of silicon in an excited state. [1]

   2-7-5

4. Write the empirical formula for the compound C_8H_{18}. [1]

   C4 H9

Day 18: continue.

Base your answers to questions 5 through 7 on the information below.

A substance is a solid at 15°C. A student heated a sample of the solid substance and recorded the temperature at one-minute intervals in the data table below.

Time (min)	0	1	2	3	4	5	6	7	8	9	10	11	12
Temperature (°C)	15	32	46	53	53	53	53	53	53	53	53	60	65

5. Based on the data table, what is the melting point of this substance? [1]

58°c

6. What is the evidence that the average kinetic energy of the particles of this substance is increasing during the first three minutes [1]

The temeperture increase during the first three minutes

7. The heat of fusion for this substance is 122 joules per gram. How many joules of heat are needed to melt 7.50 grams of this substance at it's melting? [1]

Day 18: continue.

Base your answers to questions 8 through 10 on the information below.

Naturally Occurring Isotopes of Sulfur.

Isotopes	Atomic Mass (atomic mass unit, u)	Natural Abundance (%)
^{32}S	31.97	94.93
^{33}S	32.97	0.76
^{34}S	33.97	4.29
^{36}S	35.97	0.02

8. State, in terms of the number of subatomic particles, one similarity and one difference between the atoms of these isotopes of sulfur. [1]

9. In the space below, draw a Lewis electron-dot diagram for an atom of sulfur-33. [1]

They all have the same number of protons

10. In the space below, show a correct numerical setup for calculating the atomic mass of sulfur. [1]

Day 18

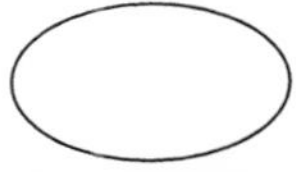

Stop. Correct your answers and note how many correct **Points**

Day 18: Answers and Explanations

1. 1 point — Acceptable response include, but are not limited to:

Group 1 elements have high chemical reactivity
Group 1 elements bond easily with other elements
Group 1 elements have oxidation state of +1

2. 1 point

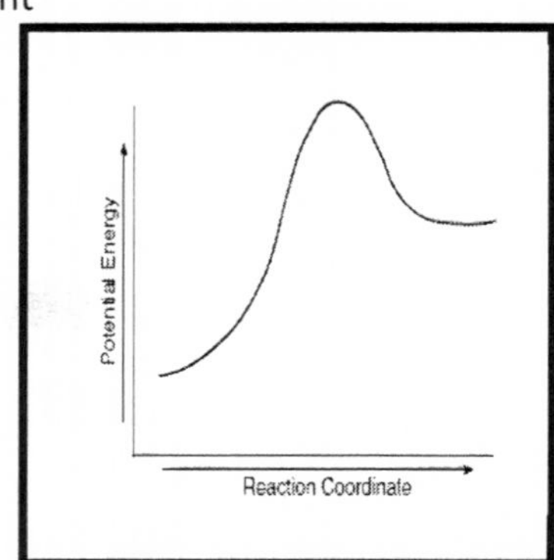

Note: Reaction is endothermic because energy (182.6 KJ) is left of arrow

Recall: energy diagram for endothermic must start low (reactants) and ends Higher (products)

Your curve may vary slightly but must show lower reactant and higher product.

3. 1 point — Acceptable configuration includes, but are not limited to :

2 – 8 – 3 – 1
2 – 7 – 5

Note: Numbers in your configuration must add up to 14, but arranged differently from the Periodic Table configuration for silicon (Si)

4. 1 point — $\mathbf{C_4H_9}$

Recall: empirical formula is the simplest ratio in which the atoms in a molecular formula are combined.

5. 1 point — **53°C**

Recall: a solid melt at a constant temperature
Note: The only constant temperature is (53°C)

Day 18: Answers and Explanations

6. 1 point — Acceptable responses includes, but are not limited to:

The **temperature during the first three minute increases.**

Recall: as temperature increases, so too is the average kinetic energy

Note: From the Table, temperature increases from 15°C to 53°C in the first three minutes

7. 1 point — **915 J**

Note: This is a heat calculation problem
Recall: Heat equations are on Table T
Use heat of fusion equation: q = m Hf
Setup and *solve:* Heat (q) = (7.5)(122) = **915 J**

8. 1 point — Acceptable responses includes, but are not limited to:
Similarity *They all have* ***same number of protons***
Difference: *They have* ***different number of neutrons.***

Recall: Isotope is defined as atoms of the same element with same number of protons but different number of neutrons.

9. 1 point

$\cdot\overset{\cdot\cdot}{\underset{\cdot}{S}}:$

Recall: A Lewis electron-dot structure must show the symbol of the atom (S) and dots equal to the number of its valance electrons (6).

10. 1 point — Acceptable setup includes, but are not limited to:
(.9493 x 32) + (.0076 x 33) + (.0429 x 34) + (.0002 x 36)

$$\frac{(94 \times 32) + (.76 \times 33) + (4.29 \times 34) + (.02 \times 36)}{100}$$

Note: Setup must show the addition of all the products of (decimal of each percent x the mass #)

Day 19: 15 Multiple Choice Questions
15 points ***Part A and B-1 Practice***

Start: Answer all questions on this day before stopping.

1. An atom in the ground state has seven valance electrons. The atom could be an atom of which element?

(1) calcium
(2) fluorine
(3) oxygen
(4) sodium

2. Which statement identifies the element arsenic?

(1) Arsenic has atomic number of 33.
(2) Arsenic has a melting point of 84 K.
(3) An atom of arsenic in the ground state has eight valance electrons.
(4) An atom of arsenic in the ground state has a radius of 146 pm..

3. What is the number of electrons in an atom of potassium?

(1) 18
(2) 19
(3) 20
(4) 39

4. Which statement describes a chemical property of hydrogen gas?

(1) Hydrogen gas burns in air
(2) Hydrogen gas is colorless
(3) Hydrogen gas has a density of 0.000 9 g/cm^3 at STP
(4) Hydrogen gas has a boiling point of 20. K at standard pressure.

5. Which unit can be used to express solution concentration?

(1) J/mol
(2) L/mol
(3) mol/L
(4) mol/s

6. Given the equation representing a system at equilibrium:

$$H_2O(s) < ===== > H_2O(l)$$

At which temperature does this equilibrium exist at 101.3 kilopascals?

(1) 0 K
(2) 0°C
(3) 32 K
(4) 273°C

7. Which metal is more active than Ni and less active then Zn?

(1) Cu
(2) Cr
(3) Mg
(4) Pb

8. Which list of nuclear emissions is arranged in order from the least penetrating power to the greatest penetrating power?

(1) alpha particle, beta particle, gamma ray
(2) alpha particle, gamma ray, beta particle
(3) gamma ray, beta particle, alpha particle
(4) beta particle, alpha particle, gamma ray

9. Which compound releases hydroxide ions in an aqueous solution?

(1) CH_3COOH
(2) CH_3OH
(3) HCl
(4) KOH

10. At 20.°C, a 1.2 gram sample of Mg ribbon reacts rapidly with 10.0 millimeters of 1.0 M HCl(aq). Which change in conditions would have caused the reaction to proceed more slowly?

(1) increasing the initial temperature to 25°C
(2) decreasing the concentration of HCl(aq) to 0.1 M
(3) using 1.2 g of powdered Mg
(4) using 2.4 g of Mg ribbon

11. Which compound is least soluble in water at 6.0°C?

(1) $KClO_3$
(2) KNO_3
(3) NaCl
(4) NH_4Cl

12. Which electron configuration represents an atom in an excited state?

(1) 2 – 7
(2) 2 – 6 – 2
(3) 2 – 8 – 1
(4) 2 – 8 – 8 – 1

13. Which two radioisotopes have the same decay mode?

(1) ^{37}Ca and ^{53}Fe
(2) ^{220}Fr and ^{60}Co
(3) ^{37}K and ^{42}K
(4) ^{99}Tc and ^{19}Ne

Day 19: continue.

14. The graph below represents the relationship between temperature and time as heat is added to a sample of H_2O.

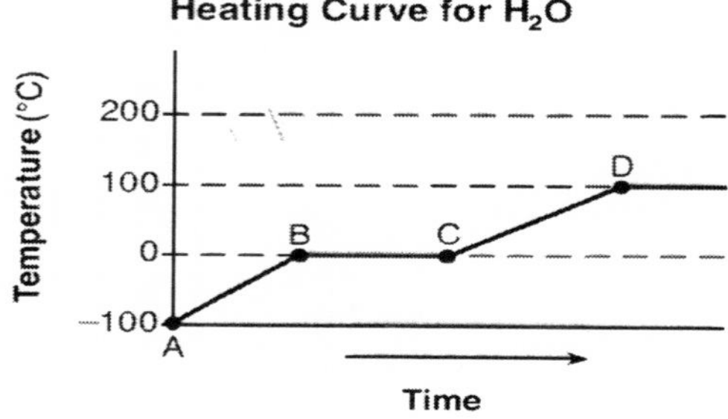

Which statement correctly describes the energy of the particles of the sample during interval BC ?

(1) Potential energy decreases and average kinetic energy increases
(2) Potential energy increases and average kinetic energy decreases
(3) Potential energy increases and average kinetic energy remains the same.
(4) Potential energy remains the same and average kinetic energy increases.

15. Given the balanced equation representing a reaction:

$C_3H_8(g) + 5O_2(g) \longrightarrow 3CO_2(g) + 4H_2O(l)$

What is the total number of moles of $O_2(g)$ required for the complete combustion of 1.5 moles of $C_3H_8(g)$?

(1) 0.30 mol
(2) 1.5 mol
(3) 4.5 mol
(4) 7.5 mol

Day 19

Stop. Correct your answers and note how many correct **Points**

Day 19: Answers and Explanations

1. 2 *Look* on the Periodic Table for configuration of each atom.
Note: Last number in configuration is the number of valance e-

2. 1 *Note:* This is the only choice that gives a correct information for As.

Note: Use the Periodic Table and Table S to check each info.

3. 2 *Recall:* Number of electrons (19) = atomic number of K (19)

4. 1 *Recall:* A chemical property depends on interaction with another substance.

Relate: Burning is chemical property because it requires interaction with (oxygen)

5. 3 *Note:* Molarity equation is on Table T

$$\text{molarity} = \frac{\text{moles } (\textbf{mol}) \text{ of solute}}{\text{Liter } (\textbf{L}) \text{ of solution}} = \frac{\text{mol}}{\text{L}}$$

6. 2 *Note:* The equation represents the melting of ice.
Recall: Ice melts at 0°C (273 K)

7. 2 *Note:* Relative reactivity of metals is shown on Table J:
Note: According to Table J:
Cr is more active (higher up) than Ni
Cr is less active (lower down) than Zn

8. **1** *Note:* The correct choice is a fact about penetrating power of nuclear particles

9. **4** *Recall*: Hydroxide (OH-) are produced by bases.
Note: Bases(such as KOH) are listed on Table L

Day 19: Answers and Explanations

10. **2** *Note*: Of all the changes to the reaction given as choices, a decrease in temp is the change that will produce slower rate (proceed slower).
All other changes will produce faster rates of reaction

11. **1** *Note*: Table G shows solubility of substances
Note: At any given temperature, the substance closest to bottom is the least soluble at that temperature.
Note: At 6.0°C, $KClO_3$ curve is the closest to the bottom

12. **2** *Recall*: an excited state configuration is not the same as what's on the Periodic Table for a given element.
Note: The correct choice has 10 e- = # of e- in a neon atom. But the configuration is differently arranged from one given on Periodic Table for a ground state Ne.

13. **1** *Recall*: Decay mode are given on Table N
Note: According to Table N, both Ca-37 and Fe-53 decay by emitting a positron (β+)

14. **3** *Note:* During BC, temperature is constant (therefore, no change in average kinetic energy)
Recall: When kinetic energy is constant, potential energy changes.

15. **4** *Note:* This is a mole proportion problem

Setup mole proportion to solve:

$$1\,C_3H_8(g) \;+\; 5O_2(g) \;\text{---->}\; 3CO_2(g) \;+\; 4H_2O(l)$$

$$\mathbf{1.5} \qquad\qquad \boldsymbol{x}$$

$$\frac{1}{\mathbf{1.5}} = \frac{5}{\boldsymbol{x}} \qquad \boldsymbol{x} = (\mathbf{1.5})(5) = \mathbf{7.5\ mol}$$

Tracking your progress
If you have completed Day 11, 13, 15, 17 and 19 multiple choice question sets, you can easily check your progress and improvements in this question category.
. Go to page 211
. Plot and graph the number of points you got correct on each of the days using the second graph on the page (the 15-point graph)

Day 20: Constructed Response Questions
10 points *Part B-2 and C Practice*

Start: Answer all questions on this day before stopping.

Base your answers to questions 1 and 2 on the information below.

In 1987, J.J. Thompson demonstrated in an experiment that cathode rays were deflected by an electric field. This suggested that cathode rays were composed of negatively charged particles found in all atoms. Thomson concluded that the atom was a positively charged sphere of almost uniform density in which negatively charged particles were embedded. The total negative charge in an atom was balanced by the positive charge, making the atom electrically neutral.

In the early 1900's, Ernest Rutherford bombarded a very thin sheet of gold foil with alpha particles. After interpreting the results of the gold foil experiment, Rutherford proposed a more sophisticated model of the atom.

1. State one conclusion from Rutherford's experiment that contradicts one conclusion made by Thomson. [1]

The nucles is Small and Positively Charged

2. State one aspect of the modern model of the atom that agrees with a conclusion made by Thomson. [1]

Number of negative equal the positively

Base your answers to questions 3 through 5 on the information below.

Some dry chemicals can be used to put out forest fires. One of these chemicals is $NaHCO_3$. When $NaHCO_3(s)$ is heated, one of the products is $CO_2(g)$, as shown in the balanced equation below.

$$2NaHCO_3(s) + \text{heat} \longrightarrow Na_2CO_3(s) + H_2O(g) + CO_2(g)$$

3. In the space in your answer booklet, show a correct numerical setup for calculating the percent composition by mass of carbon in the product, Na_2CO_3. [1]

4. Identify the type of chemical reaction represented by this equation. [1]

Endothermic

5. Determine, the total number of moles of $CO_2(g)$ produced when 7.0 moles of $NaHCO_3(s)$ is completely reacted. [1]

Day 20: continue.

Base your answer to questions 6 through 8 on the information below.

During a bread-making process, glucose is converted to ethanol and carbon dioxide, causing the bread dough to rise. Zymase, an enzyme produced by yeast, is a catalyst needed for this reaction.

6. Balance the equation below for the reaction that causes bread dough to rise, using the smallest whole-number coefficients. [1]

$$\_\_\_ \; C_6H_{12}O_6 \xrightarrow{\text{zymase}} \underline{2}\, C_2H_5OH + \underline{2}\, CO_2$$

7. In the space in your answer booklet, draw a structural formulas for the alcohol formed in this reaction. [1]

H H
| |
H - C - C - OH
| |
H H

8. State the effect of zymase on the activation energy for this reaction. [1]

lower activation energy for reaction

9. Explain, in terms of collision theory, why the rate of a chemical reaction increases with an increase in temperature. [1]

10. Base on the Periodic Table, explain why chlorine and bromine have similar chemical properties [1]

Br & Cl have the Same number of Valance eletrons.

Day 20

Stop. Correct your answers and note how many correct **Points**

Day 20: Answers and Explanations

1. 1 point

Acceptable responses include, but are not limited to:

The nucleus is small and positively charged (not the whole atom)

The atom is mostly empty space (Not a uniform density with negative charges embedded throughout)

Note: These conclusions from Rutherford's Gold foil experiment contradicts conclusions made by JJ Thompson.

2. 1 point

Acceptable responses include, but are not limited to:

The total number of electrons is equal to the total positive to make atom neutral.

Number of negative equals number of positive

3. 1 point

Acceptable setups includes, but are not limited to:

$$\% C = \frac{12}{106} \times 100 \quad or \quad \frac{1200}{106}$$

Note: Percent composition equation is on Table T

$$\% C = \frac{\text{Total mass of C}}{\text{Formula mass of } Na_2CO_3} \times 100$$

4. 1 point

Acceptable responses include, but are not limited to:

Endothermic

Note: heat is on left (reactant side) of the equation

Decomposition:

Note: Equation shows the breaking up of $NaHCO_3$ into smaller substances

Day 20: Answers and Explanations

5\. 1 point **3.5 moles**

Note: this is a mole proportion problem:

$2\ NaHCO_3(s) \ \text{---}> 1CO_2(g)$

7 ***x***

$$\frac{2}{7} = \frac{1}{x} \qquad x = 3.5 \text{ moles}$$

6\. 1 point $\_\_C_6H_{12}O_6$ -------> $\underline{\mathbf{2}}\ C_2H_5OH + \underline{\mathbf{2}}CO_2$

Recall: a balanced equation must show conservation of atoms.

Number of each atom on both sides must be the same.

Note: The correct coefficients allow there to be 6 C, 12 H, and 6 O atoms on each side of the equation .

7\. 1 point

```
    H   H
    |   |
H – C – C – OH
    |   |
    H   H
```

Note: The position of the OH may vary

8\. 1 point Acceptable responses include, but are not limited to:

Zymase (a catalyst) lowers activation energy for the reaction.
Zymase provides alternate pathways for the reaction.

9\. 1 point Acceptable responses include, but are not limited to:

There is an increase in the kinetic energy of the particles.
There is increase in the frequency of collisions or particles.

10\. 1 point Acceptable responses include, but are not limited to:

Cl and Br are in the same Group (17).
Cl and Br are halogens
Cl and Br have the same number of valance electrons
Cl and Br have similar oxidation state.

A + B → AB
Synthesis

AB → A + B
decomposition

Day 21: 20 Multiple Choice Questions

20 points ***Part A and B-1 Practice***

Start: Answer all questions on this day before stopping.

1. Which subatomic particles are located in the nucleus of a neon atom?

(1) electrons and positrons
(2) electrons and neutrons
(3) protons and neutrons
(4) protons and electrons

2. An atom of argon rarely bonds to an atom of another element because an argon atom has

(1) 8 valance electrons
(2) 2 electrons in the first shell
(3) 3 electron shells
(4) 22 neutrons

3. Bronze contains 90 to 95 percent copper and 5 to 10 percent tin. Because these percentages can vary, bronze is classified as

(1) a compound
(2) an element
(3) a mixture
(4) a substance

4. Which compound has hydrogen bonding between its molecules?

(1) CH_4
(2) CaH_2
(3) KH
(4) NH_3

5. At STP, which list of elements contains a solid, a liquid, and a gas?

(1) Hf, Hg, He
(2) Cr, Cl_2, C
(3) Ba, Br_2, B
(4) Se, Sn, Sr

6. The three isomers of pentane have different

(1) formula mass
(2) empirical formula
(3) molecular mass
(4) structural formula

7. Which molecule contains a nonpolar covalent bond?

(1) O = C = O
(2) C = O
(3) Br – Br
(4)
```
     Cl
     |
Cl – C – Cl
     |
     Cl
```

Day 21: continue.

8. Which formula represents an electrolyte?

(1) CH_3OCH_3
(2) CH_3OH
(3) CH_3COOH
(4) C_2H_5CHO

9. Which equation represents a fusion reaction?

(1) $H_2O(g) \text{ --------------> } H_2O(l)$
(2) $C(s) + O_2(g) \text{ ------> } CO_2(g)$
(3) ${}^{2}_{1}H + {}^{3}_{1}H \text{ ---------> } {}^{4}_{2}He + {}^{1}_{0}n$
(4) ${}^{235}_{92}U + {}^{1}_{0}n \text{ --------> } {}^{142}_{56}Ba + {}^{91}_{36}Kr + 3{}^{1}_{0}n$

10. A sample of a substance containing only magnesium and chlorine was tested in the laboratory and was found to be composed of 74.5% chlorine by mass. If the total mass of the sample was 190.2 grams, what was the mass of the magnesium?

(1) 24.3 g
(2) 48.5 g
(3) 70.9 g
(4) 142 g

11. In which process does a solid changes directly into a vapor?

(1) condensation
(2) sublimation
(3) deposition
(4) solidification

12. When an Arrhenius acid dissolves in water, the only positive ion in the solution is

(1) H+
(2) Li+
(3) Na+
(4) K+

13. Types of nuclear reactions include fission, fusion, and

(1) single replacement
(2) neutralization
(3) oxidation-reduction
(4) transmutation

14. When an atom becomes a positive ion, the radius of the atom

(1) decreases, because it has lost electrons
(2) decreases, because it has gained electrons
(3) increases, because it has lost electrons
(4) remains the same

Day 21: continue.

15. Which structural formula is correct for 2-methyl-3-pentanol?

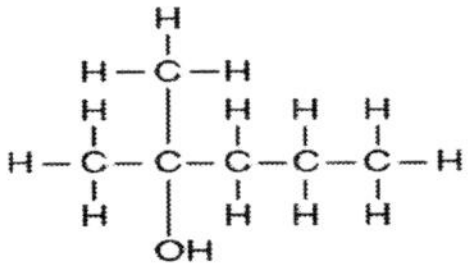

(1)

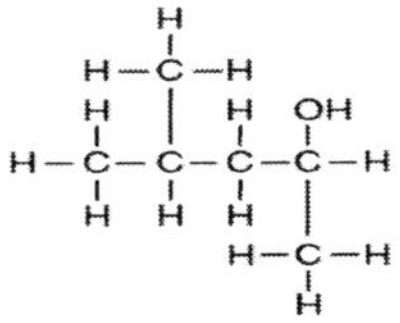

(3)

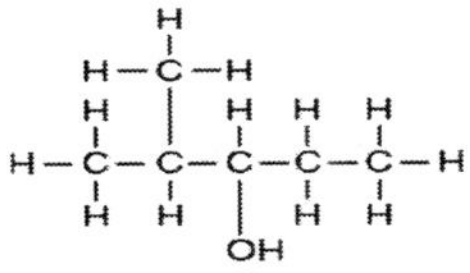

(2)

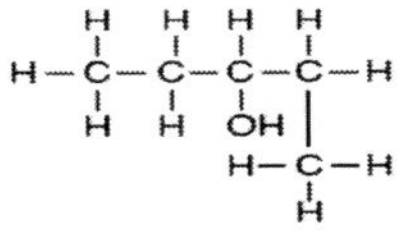

(4)

16. The atomic mass of element A is 63.6 atomic mass units. The only naturally occurring isotopes of element A are A-63 and A-65. The percent abundances in a naturally occurring sample of element A are closest to

(1) 31% A-63 and 69% A-65
(2) 50% A-63 and 50% A-65
(3) 69% A-63 and 31% A-65
(4) 100% A-63 and 0% A-65

17. Given the balance equation:

$$4Fe(s) + 3O_2(g) \longrightarrow 2Fe_2O_3(s) + 1640KJ$$

Which phrase best describes this reaction?

(1) endothermic with $\Delta H = +1640$ KJ
(2) endothermic with $\Delta H = -1640$ KJ
(3) exothermic with $\Delta H = +1640$ KJ
(4) exothermic with $\Delta H = -1640$ KJ

Day 21: continue.

18. Which indicator is yellow in a solution with a pH of 9.8?

(1) methyl orange
(2) bromthymol blue
(3) bromcresol green
(4) thymol blue

19. What is the chemical formula for sodium sulfate?

(1) Na_2SO_3
(2) Na_2SO_4
(3) $NaSO_3$
(4) $NaSO_4$

20. The decay of which radioisotope can be used to estimate the age of the fossilized remains of an insect?

(1) Rn-222
(2) I-131
(3) Co-60
(4) C-14

Day 21

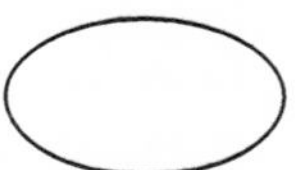

Stop. Correct your answers and note how many correct **Points**

Day 21: Answers and Explanations

1. **3** *Recall:* A nucleus of any atom contains protons and neutrons

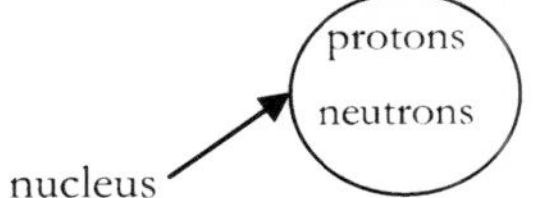

2. **1** *Note:* This choice is a fact about the noble gases (Group 18 element) such as argon. (See Periodic Table)
The 8 valance electrons give noble gases full and stable configurations. Therefore, they rarely bond with other atoms.

3. **3** *Note:* 90 – 95% stated in question suggest varying composition:
Recall: Compositions of ***Mixtures*** can vary

4. **4** *Recall:* hydrogen bonding (a strong intermolecular forces) exists between the molecules of NH_3 , H_2O and HF

5. **1** *Recall:* **Hg** (and Br) are the only **liquid** elements
He is a noble **gas** (because it is in Group 18)
Hf is a transition metal (all transition metals, except Hg, exist as **solid.)**

6. **4** *Recall:* isomers are organic compounds with same molecular formula BUT different structural formulas

7. **3** *Recall:* Nonpolar bonds are found between the atoms of two of the same nonmetal atoms (Br – Br)

8. **3** *Recall:* Acids (Table K), bases (Table L), and salts are electrolytes.
CH_3COOH is an acid (See Table K)

Day 21: Answers and Explanations

9. **3** *Recall:* Fusion is a nuclear process of joining two smaller nuclei of H to form a larger nucleus of He.

10. **2** *Note:* If the sample contains 74.5 % by mass of chlorine, the remaining percent of 25.5 % will be of the mass of Mg

Relate: the mass of Mg in sample is, therefore, 25.5 % of 190.2 g.

Calculate : 25.5 % of 190.2 g to get mass of Magnesium (Mg).
0.255 x 190.2 = **48.5 g**

11. **2** *Recall:* sublimation is a phase change of *solid* -----> *gas*

12. **1** *Note:* correct choice is a fact related to all Arrhenius acids

13. **4** *Recall* that the common types of nuclear reactions are :

Nuclear energy reactions: fission
fusion

Natural Transmutation: alpha decay
beta decay
position emission.

Artificial Transmutation

14. **1** *Recall:* A positive ion is formed when an atom loses its valance e-.
Note: The + ion is always smaller because the atom also loses the entire valance shell.

15. **2** *Note:* This structure is correct because it shows:

a methyl (CH_3) group on the 2nd C atom (2-methyl)

an -OH group on the 3rd C (3-pentanol)

The long chain has 5 C atoms (pent-)

Day 21: Answers and Explanations

16. **3** *Note:* The atomic mass (63.5g) is closer to 63g than to 65g.

Relate: The bigger percentage of the isotopes must have a mass of 63.g (as given in choice 3)

17. **4** *Note:* The equation is exothermic because energy is on the right

Recall: exothermic reactions have $-\Delta H$ value (see Table I)

18. **1** *Note:* According to Table M:

Methyl orange changes from red to yellow from pH of 3.2.

It will stay yellow in any solution that has a pH greater than 4.

19. **2** *Recall:* a correct formula must show the correct atom symbols and the correct number of each atom (subscript)

	sodium	*sulfate*
Use Periodic Table and Table E to obtain correct symbols and charges	Na^{+1}	$(SO_4)^{2-}$
Use criss-cross method to obtain appropriate subscripts	Na_2SO_4	

20. **4** *Recall:* C-14 (along with C-12) is commonly used in determining age of fossilized organisms.

Day 22: Constructed Response Questions
10 points — *Part B-2 and C Practice*

Start: Answer all questions on this day before stopping.

Base your answers to question 1 through 3 on the information below.

The compound $NH_4Br(s)$ and $NH_3(g)$ are soluble in water. Solubility data for $NH_4Br(s)$ in water are listed in the table below.

Solubility of NH_4Br in H_2O

Temperature (°C)	Mass of NH_4Br per 100. g of H_2O (g)
0	60.
20.	75.
40.	90.
60.	105
80.	120
100.	135

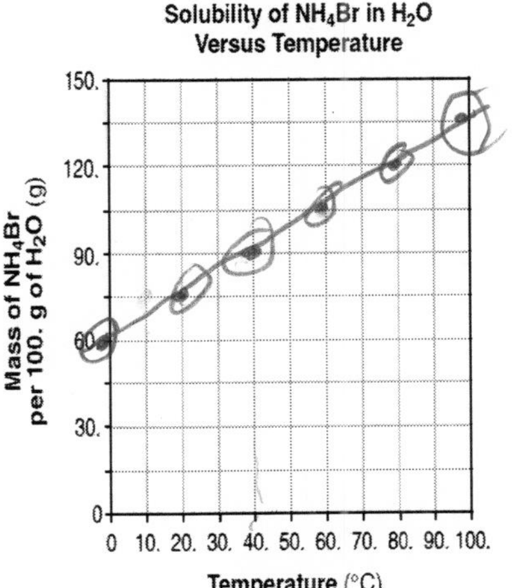

1. On the grid to the right, plot the data from the data table. Circle and connect the points. [1]

2. Determine the total mass of $NH_4Br(s)$ that must be dissolved in 200. grams of H_2O at 60.°C to produce a saturated solution. [1]

210 grams

3. Compare the solubility of $NH_4Br(s)$ and $NH_3(g)$, each in 100. grams of H_2O, as temperature increases at standard pressure. Your response must include both $NH_4Br(s)$ and $NH_3(g)$. [1]

Solabilty of NH4Br goes up and

Day 22: continue.

Base your answers to questions 4 through 6 on the balanced equation below.

$$2H_2O \text{ -----> } 2\,H_2 + O_2$$

4. What type of reaction does this equation represent? [1]

Decomposition

5. How does the balanced chemical equation show the Law of Conservation of Mass? [1]

The atom is equal to both side

6. What is the total number of moles of O_2 produced when 8 moles of H_2O is completely consumed? [1]

Base your answers to questions 7 through 10 on the information below.

A safe level of fluoride ions is added to many public drinking water supplies. Fluoride ions have been found to help prevent tooth decay. Another common source of fluoride ions is toothpaste. One of the fluoride compounds used in toothpaste is tin(II) fluoride.
A town located downstream from a chemical plant was concerned about fluoride ions from the plant leaking into its drinking water. According to the Environmental Protection Agency, the fluoride ion concentration in drinking water cannot exceed 4 ppm. The town hired a chemist to analyze its water. The chemist determined that a 175-gram sample of the town's water contains 0.00250 gram of fluoride ions.

7. In the space below, draw a Lewis electron-dot diagram for a fluoride ion. [1]

:F: -1

Day 22: continue.

8. What is the chemical formula for tin (II) fluoride? [1]

SnF_2

9. How many parts per million of fluoride ions are present in the analyzed sample? [1]

10. Is the town's drinking water safe to drink? Support your decision using information in the passage and your calculated fluoride level in question 9. [1]

No, because the Connection of Fl ion is greater than the limit Connection

Day 22

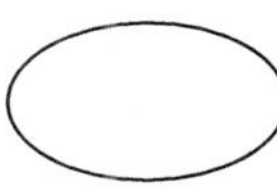

Stop. Correct your answers and note how many correct **Points**

Day 22: Answers and Explanations

1. 1 point **For plotting and graphing the data**

Example of a 1-point graph for question 1

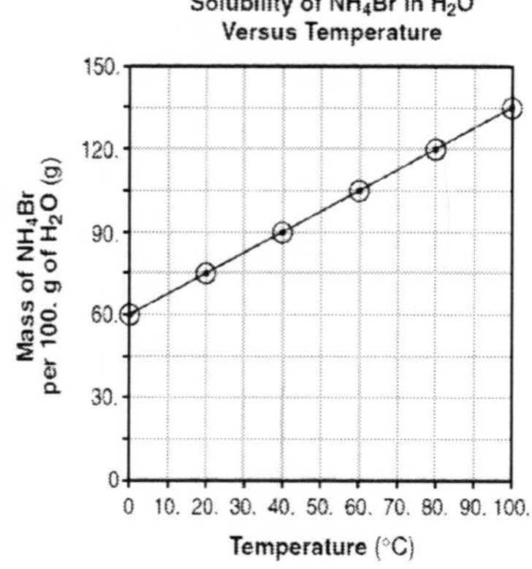

Graph may vary

2. 1 point **210g**.

Since this answer depends on your graph, allow point for grams that is consistent with your graph.

3. 1 point Acceptable responses include, but are not limited to:

As temperature increases:

solubility of $NH_4Br(s)$ increases while the solubility of $NH_3(g)$ decreases.

Solubility of $NH_4Br(s)$ goes up and the solubility of $NH_3(g)$ goes down

Recall these facts: As temp ↑ most solid become more soluble gases become less soluble

4. 1 point Acceptable response includes, but are not limited to:
Decomposition
Analysis

Recall: in decomposition reactions, a compound reactant (H_2O) is broken down into smaller substances products (H_2 and O_2)

Day 22: Answers and Explanations

5. 1 point

Acceptable responses include, but are not limited to:
The number of each atom is equal on both sides.
Mass of reactants is equal to mass of products

Recall: Law of Conservation of Mass states that atoms are neither created nor destroyed.

6. 1 point

4

Note: this is a mole proportion problem

Solve by setting up mole proportion.

$2H_2O$ -----> $2\ H_2$ + $1O_2$

8 ***x*** <--------- *From follow up question*

$$\frac{2}{\mathbf{8}} = \frac{1}{\mathbf{x}} \qquad x = \mathbf{4\ moles}$$

7. 1 point

$:\ddot{\underset{\cdot\cdot}{F}}:$ -1

Recall: Lewis electron-dot diagram for a negative ion must show the symbol of the ion and 8 dots around it.

Exception is a a negative hydrogen ion (H-) , which can only have 2 dots around it ($H:^{-}$)

8. 1 point

SnF_2

Use criss-cross method to determine correct formula.

tin (**II**) fluoride

Sn^{2+} F^{1-} Recall: (**II**) means **+2** charge for Sn

SnF_2

Day 22: Answers and Explanations

9. 1 point **14.3 ppm**

Note: Use part per million equation on Table T to calculate.

$$ppm = \frac{\text{Grams of solute}}{\text{Grams of solution}} \times 100000$$

$$ppm = \frac{0.00250}{(175\text{ g} + .00250)} \times 1000000 = \mathbf{14.3\ ppm}$$

10. 1 point Acceptable responses include, but are not limited to:

No, because the ppm concentration of F- ion (14.3 ppm) exceeds the safe limit of F- ion (4 ppm) set by Environmental Protection Agency.

No, because the concentration of fluoride ion is greater than the safe limit concentration

Day 23: 20 Multiple Choice Questions
20 points ***Part A and B-1 Practice***

Start: Answer all questions on this day before stopping.

1. Compared to a proton, an electron has
   (1) greater quantity of charge and the same sign
   (2) greater quantity of charge and the opposite sign
   (3) the same quantity of charge and the same sign
   (4) the same quantity of charge and the opposite sign

2. Which two notation represents atoms that are isotopes of the same element?
   (1) $^{121}_{50}Sn$ and $^{119}_{50}Sn$
   (2) $^{121}_{50}Sn$ and $^{121}_{50}Sn$
   (3) $^{19}_{8}O$ and $^{19}_{9}F$
   (4) $^{39}_{17}Cl$ and $^{39}_{19}K$

3. Which substance can be decomposed by a chemical change?
   (1) calcium
   (2) potassium
   (3) copper
   (4) ammonia

4. Based on Reference Table S, the atoms of which of these elements have the strongest attraction for electrons in a chemical bond?
   (1) N
   (2) Na
   (3) P
   (4) Pt

5. Which Period 4 element has the most metallic properties?
   (1) As
   (2) Br
   (3) Ge
   (4) Se

6. What is the total number of pairs of electrons shared in a molecule of N_2?
   (1) one pair
   (2) two pairs
   (3) three pairs
   (4) four pair

7. Which statement best describes the shape and volume of an aluminum cylinder at STP?
   (1) It has definite shape and a definite volume
   (2) It has definite shape and no definite volume
   (3) It has no definite shape and a definite volume
   (4) It has no definite shape and no definite volume

Day 23: continue.

8. A compound is made up of iron and oxygen, only. The ratio of iron ions and oxide ions is 2:3 in this compound. The IUPAC name for this compound is

   (1) triiron dioxide
   (2) iron (II) oxide
   (3) iron (III) oxide
   (4) iron trioxide

9. A substance is described as an electrolyte because

   (1) it has a high melting point
   (2) it contains covalent bonds
   (3) its aqueous solution conducts an electrical current
   (4) its aqueous solution has a pH value of 7

10. Systems in nature tend to under changes toward

   (1) lower energy and lower entropy
   (2) lower energy and higher entropy
   (3) higher energy and lower entropy
   (4) higher energy and higher entropy

11. Compared to a 0.1 M aqueous solution of NaCl, a 0.8 M aqueous solution of NaCl has a

   (1) higher boiling point and a higher freezing point
   (2) higher boiling point and a lower freezing point
   (3 lower boiling point and a higher freezing point
   (4) lower boiling point and a lower freezing point

12. An atom of oxygen is in an excited state. When an electron in this atom moves from the third shell to the second shell, energy is

   (1) emitted by the nucleus
   (2) emitted by the electron
   (3) absorbed by the nucleus
   (4) absorbed by the electron

Day 23: continue.

13. Which chemical equation is correctly balanced?

(1) $H_2(g)$ + $O_2(g)$ -----> $H_2O(g)$
(2) $N_2(g)$ + $H_2(g)$ ------> $NH_3(g)$
(3) $2NaCl(s)$ ---------> $Na(s)$ + $Cl_2(g)$
(4) $2KCl(s)$ -----> $2K(s)$ + $Cl_2(g)$

14. Which type of bond is found in sodium bromide?

(1) covalent
(2) hydrogen
(3) ionic
(4) metallic

15. Which Lewis electron dot is correct for CO_2?

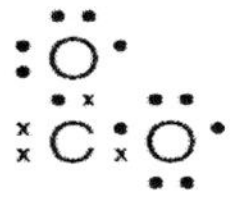

(1)  (3)

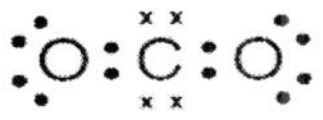

(2) 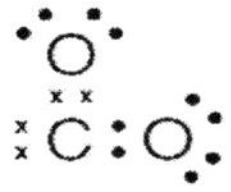 (4)

16. Two sample of gold that have different temperatures are placed in contact with one another. Heat will flow spontaneously from a sample of gold at 60°C to a sample of gold that has a temperature of

(1) 50°C
(2) 60°C
(3) 70°C
(4) 80°C

Day 23: continue.

17. Given the reaction system in a closed container at equilibrium and at a temperature of 298 K:

$N_2O_4(g)$ < ===== > $2NO_2(g)$

The measureable quantities of the gases at equilibrium must be

(1) decreasing
(2) increasing
(3) equal
(4) constant

18. A solution contains 35 grams of KNO_3 dissolved in 100 grams of water at 40°C. How much more KNO_3 would have to be added to make it a saturated solution?

(1) 29 g
(2) 24 g
(3) 12 g
(4) 4 g

19. Which Kelvin temperature is equivalent to -24°C?

(1) 226 K
(2) 249 K
(3) 273 K
(4) 297 K

20. Given the formula

```
    H  H  H  O
    |  |  |  ||     H
H - C - C - C - C - N /
    |  |  |         \ H
    H  H  H
```

The compound is classified as

(1) an aldehyde
(2) an amide
(3) an amine
(4) a ketone

Day 23

Stop. Correct your answers and note how many correct **Points**

Day 23: Answers and Explanations

1. **4** *Recall:* A Proton has a +1 charge
An electron has a -1 charge (opposite sign (-), same quantity (1)

2. **1** *Recall:* Isotope symbols must have:
Same bottom numbers (corresponding to the atomic number of the element

Different top numbers (different mass numbers of the isotopes)

3. **4** *Recall:* Compounds can be decomposed.
Note: NH_3 (ammonia) is a compound b/c it is composed of two different atoms.
Note All other choices are elements (elements cannot be decomposed)

4. **1** *Recall:* Electronegativity value (Table S) measures an atom's ability to attract electrons during bonding.
Element with the highest electronegativity value (N) has the strongest attraction

5. **3** *Recall:* Within a Period, element farthest LEFT has strongest metallic properties and weakest nonmetallic properties
Note: Ge is the farthest Left of the Periodic Table of all the choices given

6. **3** *Recall:* N_2 has a structure of $N \equiv N$.
Recall: Each bond (–) is composed of 2 electrons (1 pair of e-)
Relate: The triple bonds in N_2 consist of three pairs of electrons (6 total electrons)

7. **1** *Note:* Aluminum is a solid metal at STP.
The correct choice reflects properties (definition) of a solid

8. **3** *Note:* The formula of this compound with 2 : 3 ratio MUST be

$$Fe_2O_3$$

The name of this compound must be Iron(III) oxide

Day 23: Answers and Explanations

9. **3** *Note:* The correct choice is a definition of an electrolyte.

10. **2** *Note:* The correct choice is a fact related to systems in nature

11. **2** *Note:* You are comparing a higher NaCl solution concentration (0.8 M) to a lower concentration (0.1 M).

    Recall: The higher the concentration, the higher the boiling point and the lower the freezing point of a solution.

12. **2** *Note:* The electron transition in the question is from a higher shell (3rd) to a lower shell (2nd)

    Recall: Energy is released (emitted) by an electron as the electron moves from a higher to lower shell.

13. **4** *Recall:* Equation is balanced when the number of each atom is equal on both sides (demonstrates conservation)

    Note: The correct equation has 2 K and 2 Cl on both sides

14. **3** *Note:* Sodium bromide is composed of a metal (Na) and a nonmetal (Br)

    Recall: Ionic bond is formed between a metal and a nonmetal.

15. **3** *Recall:* Structure of CO_2 is O = C = O

    This Lewis structure for choice 3 is correct because:

    It shows the correct number of shared electrons

    It shows all atoms with octet (8) of electrons

16. **1** *Recall:* Heat only flows from high temp object to lower temp.

    Note: This choice is correct b/c heat will from a gold at 60°C to a gold with a lower temp (50°C)

17. **4** *Recall* these equilibrium facts:

    Concentration (measureable quantity) of substances must be ***constant.***

    Rate of forward and reveres reactions must be ***equal***

Day 23: Answers and Explanations

18. **1** *Use* Table G to determine the difference between the saturated amount of KNO_3 at 40°C and the amount of KNO_3 in the solution.

According to Table G:

The saturated amount of KNO_3 at 40°C = 64 g

Note: The amount of KNO_3 in the solution = 35 g

Subtract to get amount of KNO_3 to be be added = 29 g

19. **2** *Note:* Use Table T equation $K = {}^{\circ}C + 273$ to solve

$K = -24 + 273 =$ **249 K**

20. **2** *Compare* the functional group in the structure given to those on Reference Table R

Note: The structure has amide functional group

Day 24: Constructed Response Questions
10 points *Part B-2 and C Practice*

Start: Answer all questions on this day before stopping.

Base your answers to questions 1 through 2 on the balanced equation below.

$Fe(s) + HNO_3(aq) \text{ ----> } Fe(NO_3)_2(aq) + H_2(g)$

1. What is the total number of oxygen atoms represented in the formula of the iron compound produced? [1]

2. Explain, using information from Reference Table J, why this reaction is spontaneous.

Base your answers to questions 3 and 4 on the information below.

In a titration, 15.65 millimeters of a KOH(aq) solution exactly neutralized 10.00 millimeters of a 1.22 M HCl(aq) solution.

3. Complete the equation below for the titration reaction by writing the formula for each product. [1]

KOH + HCl ----> _____ + ______

4. In the space below, show a correct numerical setup for calculating the molarity of KOH(aq) solution. [1]

Day 24: continue.

Base your answer to questions 5 and 6 on the information below.

Electroplating is an electrolytic process used to coat metal objects with a more expensive and less reactive metal. The diagram below shows an electroplating cell that includes a battery connected to a silver bar and a metal spoon. The bar and spoon are submerged in $AgNO_3(aq)$.

An Electroplating Cell

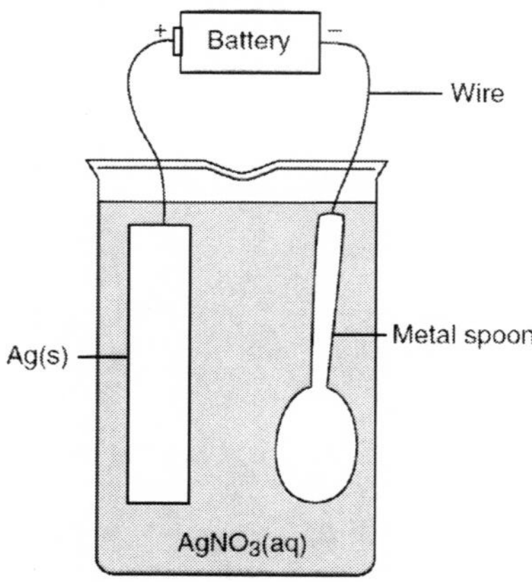

5. Explain why $AgNO_3$ is a better choice than AgCl for used in this electrolytic process. [1]

6. Explain the purpose of the battery in this cell. [1]

Day 24: continue.

Base your answers to questions 7 and 8 on the information below.

An atom has an atomic number of 9, a mass number of 19, and an electron configuration of 2 – 6 – 1.

7. What is the total number of neutrons in this atom? [1]

8. Explain why the number of electrons in the second and third shells shows that this atom is in an excited state? [1]

Base your answers to question 9 and 10 on the information below.

The balanced equation below represents the reaction between magnesium metal and hydrochloric acid to produce aqueous magnesium chloride and hydrogen gas.

$Mg(s)$ + $2HCl(aq)$ ---- > $MgCl_2(aq)$ + $H_2(g)$

A piece of Mg(s) has a volume of 0.0640 cubic centimeters. This piece of Mg(s) reacts completely with HCl(aq) to produce $H_2(g)$. The $H_2(g)$ produced has a volume of 112 millimeters and a pressure of 1.00 atmosphere at 298 K.

9. The volume of the piece of Mg(s) is expressed to what number of significant figures? [1]

10. In the space below, show a correct numerical setup for calculating the volume of the $H_2(g)$ produced if the conditions are changed to STP. [1]

Day 24

Stop. Correct your answers and note how many correct **Points**

Day 24: Answers and Explanations

1. **1 point** **6**

   Note: The iron compound produced is $Fe(NO_3)_2$

   Determine: Number of moles of O is 3 x 2 = 6

2. **1 point** Acceptable responses include, but are not limited to:

   Fe is more reactive than the H

   H on Table J is lower down than Fe

   Recall: A reaction will be spontaneous if the **single free element (Fe)** in the reaction is more reactive (higher up on Table J) than the **element in the compound (H)** it is replacing

   Fe(s) + $HNO_3(aq)$ ----> $Fe(NO_3)_2(aq) + H_2(g)$

   free element — *element being replaced*

3. **1 point** KOH + HCl ----> **$\underline{H_2O}$** + **$\underline{KCl}$**

   Recall: Products of all neutralization reactions are water (H_2O) and salt (KCl)

   Note: You can find the correct formula of the salt by replacing the H of the acid with the metal of the base

   Note how K (metal) replaces H of HCl to form KCl salt

4. **1 point** Acceptable setups include, but are not limited to:

   (1.22) (10) = M_b (15.65)

   1.22 x 10

   15.65

   Note: Titration equation is given on Table T

Day 24: Answers and Explanations

5. **1 point**

Acceptable responses include, but are not limited to:

$AgNO_3$ is better than AgCl in electrolytic cell because :

$AgNO_3$ is a soluble salt (According to Table F)

$AgNO_3$ dissolves better than AgCl

$AgNO_3$ will produce more ions in the solution

Recall: The solution in electrolytic cells must contain ions

6. **1 point**

Acceptable responses include, but are not limited to:

The battery provides electrical energy needed to force the nonspontaneous reaction in the electrolytic cell to occur.

Recall: In electrolytic cells, electrical energy (from battery) is converted to chemical energy

7. **1 point**

10

Recall: Neutrons = Mass # - Atomic # (protons)

10 = 19 - 9

8. **1 point**

Acceptable responses include, but are not limited to:

The 3rd shell only has 6 electrons (not full with 8) while the 2nd contains an electron.

The second shell should not have any electrons unless there are 8 electrons in the third shell

Day 24: Answers and Explanations

9. 1 point ***3***

Note: In the number 0.0**<u>640</u>**, the last 3 digits are significant

Recall the following rules for counting significant numbers:

.All zero to start a number (***0.0*** 640) are **NOT** significant

.All Real numbers (0.0***<u>64</u>*** 0) are significant

.If a number has a decimal point, all zeros following a real number are significant 0.0*<u>640</u>*)

10. 1 point Acceptable setups include, but are not limited to:

$$\frac{(1)(112)}{298} = \frac{(1)(V_2)}{273}$$

$$V_2 = \frac{(112)(273)}{298}$$

Note: This is a gas law problem that can be setup using the combined gas law equation on Table T:

$$\frac{P_1V_1}{T_1} = \frac{P_2V_2}{T_2}$$

Note: Factors to put in equation are as follow:

From passage	*From question*	
V_1 = 112 ml	V_2 = unknown	
P_1 = 1 atm	P_2 = 1 atm	***STP***
T_1 = 298 K	T_2 = 273	

Day 25: 20 Multiple Choice Questions
20 points ***Part A and B-1 Practice***

Start: Answer all questions on this day before stopping.

1. Which subatomic particle has a negative charge?

(1) proton
(2) electron
(3) neutron
(4) positron

2. Which statement best describes the nucleus of an aluminum atom?

(1) It has a charge of +13 and is surrounded by 10 electrons.
(2) It has a charge of +13 and is surrounded by 13 electrons.
(3) It has a charge of -13 and is surrounded by 10 electrons.
(4) It has a charge of -13 and is surrounded by 13 electrons.

3. Two different samples decomposed when heated. Only one of the samples is soluble in water. Based on this information, these two samples are

(1) both the same element
(2) two different elements
(3) both the same compound
(4) two different compounds

4. Which of these elements has the lowest melting point?

(1) Li
(2) Na
(3) K
(4) Rb

5. Which list consists of types of chemical formulas?

(1) atoms, ions, molecules
(2) metals, nonmetals, metalloids
(3) empirical, molecular, structural
(4) synthesis, decomposition, neutralization

6. Which formula represents a nonpolar molecule?

(1) H_2S
(2) HCl
(3) CH_4
(4) NH_4

7. An aqueous solution of sodium chloride is best described as a

(1) homogeneous compound
(2) homogeneous mixture
(3) heterogeneous compound
(4) heterogeneous mixture

Day 25: continue.

8. Under which conditions of temperature and pressure would helium behave most like an ideal gas?

(1) 50 K and 20 kPa
(2) 50 K and 600 kPa
(3) 750 K and 20 kPa
(4) 750 K and 600 kPa

9. Which formula represents an unsaturated hydrocarbon?

```
    H  H
    |  |
H - C - C = C - H
    |       |
    H       H
```

(1)

```
    H   H   H
    |   |   |
H - C - C - C - H
    |   |   |
    H   H   H
```

(2)

```
    H   H   H
    |   |   |
H - C - C - C - Cl
    |   |   |
    H   H   H
```

(3)

```
    H   H   O
    |   |   ||
H - C - C - C - H
    |   |
    H   H
```

(4)

10. Given the balanced equation:

$2C + 3H_2$ -----> C_2H_6

What is the total number of moles of C that must completely react to produce 2.0 moles of C_2H_6?

(1) 1.0 mol
(2) 2.0 mol
(3) 3.0 mol
(4) 4.0 mol

11. Which electron configuration represents the electrons in an atom of chlorine in an excited state.?

(1) 2 – 7 – 7
(2) 2 – 7 – 8
(3) 2 – 8 – 7
(4) 2 – 8 – 8

Day 25: continue.

12. What is the oxidation number assigned to manganese in $KMnO_4$?

(1) +7
(2) +2
(3) +3
(4) +4

13. A student tested a 0.1 M aqueous solution and made the following observations:

. conducts electricity
. turns blue litmus to red
. reacts with Zn(s) to produce gas bubbles.

Which compound could be the solute in this solution?

(1) CH_3OH
(2) LiBr
(3) HBr
(4) LiOH

14. Which equation represents a neutralization reaction?

(1) $4Fe(s) + 3O_2(g) \rightarrow 2Fe_2O_3(s)$
(2) $2H_2(g) + O_2(g) \rightarrow 2H_2O(l)$
(3) $HNO_3(aq) + KOH(aq) \rightarrow KNO_3(aq) + H_2O(l)$
(4) $AgNO_3(aq) + KCl(aq) \rightarrow KNO_3(aq) + AgCl(s)$

15. Given the balance equation representing a redox reaction:

$$2Al + 3Cu^{2+} \rightarrow 2Al^{3+} + 3Cu$$

Which statement is true about this reaction?

(1) Each Al loses 2e- and each Cu^{2+} gains 3e-
(2) Each Al loses 3e- and each Cu^{2+} gains 2e-
(3) Each Al^{3+} gains 2e- and each Cu loses 3e-
(4) Each Al^{3+} gains 3e- and each Cu loses 2e-

16. The percent composition by mass of magnesium in $MgBr_2$ (gram-formula mass = 184 grams/mole) is equal to

(1) $\frac{24}{184} \times 100$
(2) $\frac{160.}{184} \times 100$
(3) $\frac{184}{24} \times 100$
(4) $\frac{184}{160.} \times 100$

17. Given the potential energy diagram for a reaction:

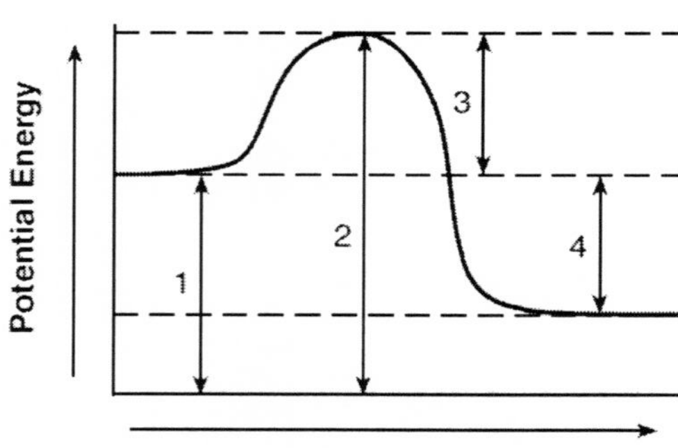

Which interval on this diagram represents the difference between the potential energy of the products and the potential energy of the reactants?

(1) 1
(2) 2
(3) 3
(4) 4

18. Given the balanced equation representing a reaction:

$CH_4(g) + 2O_2(g) \longrightarrow 2H_2O(g) + CO_2(g) + \text{heat}$

Which statement is true about energy in this reaction?

(1) The reaction is exothermic because it releases heat.
(2) The reaction is exothermic because it absorbs heat.
(3) The reaction is endothermic because it releases heat.
(4) The reaction is endothermic because it absorbs heat.

19. Which diagram represents the nucleus of an atom of $^{27}_{13}Al$?

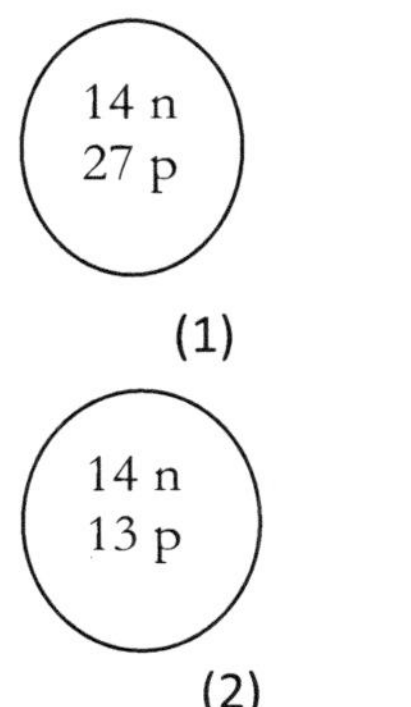

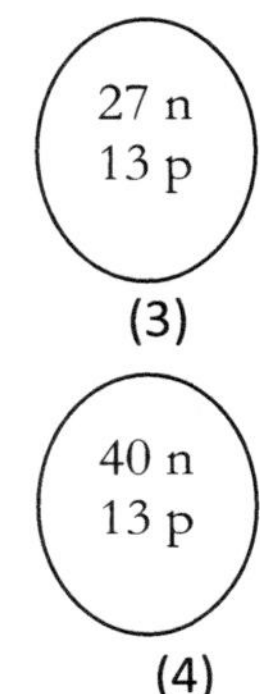

20. The chart below shows the spontaneous nuclear decay of U-238 to Th-234 to Pa-234 to U-234.

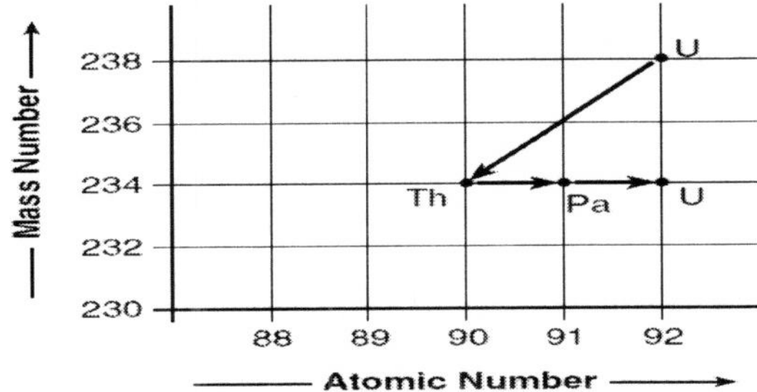

What is the correct order of nuclear decay modes for the change from U-238 to U-234?

(1) β-decay, γ decay, β-decay
(2) β-decay, β-decay, α decay
(3) α decay, α decay, β-decay
(4) α decay, β-decay, β-decay

Day 25

Stop. Correct your answers and note how many correct **Points**

Day 25: Answers and Explanations

1. **2** *Note:* key phrase "negative charge", which describes electrons

2. **2** *Note:* Nuclear charge of all Aluminum (Al) atoms is +13.
Recall: In neutral atoms: # of electrons (13) = atomic number (13)

3. **4** *Note:* The two samples are compound b/c they can be decomposed when heated
Note: The two samples are different b/c one is soluble and the other isn't
Recall: Sample of the same substance must have the same set of properties. These two samples do not have the same set of properties

4. **4** *Use* Reference Table S to compare melting points of the elements given as choices.

5. **3**

6. **3** *Recall:* A molecule is nonpolar if its structure is symmetrical.

Note: Structure of CH_4

```
    H
    |
H – C – H
    |
    H
```

is symmetrical.

7. **2** *Recall:* All aqueous solutions are homogeneous mixtures

8. **3** *Recall:* Real gases (He) behaves most like an ideal gas under High Temp (750 K) and Low Pressure (20 kPa)

9. **1** *Recall:* Unsaturated hydrocarbons are the alkenes and alkynes.
Note: the correct structure is of an alkene b/c the structure consists of *one double bonded* carbon atoms.

Day 25: Answers and Explanations

10. **4** *Setup* mole proportion to determine mole of C that must react.

$$2C + 3H_2 \text{ -----> } 1C_2H_6$$
$$x \qquad\qquad\qquad 2$$

$$\frac{2}{x} = \frac{1}{2}$$

$$x = \textbf{4 mol}$$

11. **2** *Note:* this excited state configuration is correct b/c the numbers in the configuration add up to 17 (# of electrons in Cl atom) BUT, arranged differently from the Periodic Table (ground state) configuration

12. **1** *Recall:* sum of charges in a compound must equal zero.
Note: This charge of Mn (+7) adds to charge of K (+1) and the total charge of O (-8) to equal zero.

13. **3** *Note:* the observations describe properties of acids.
Note: HBr is an acid (Use Table K)

14. **3** *Recall:* Neutralization is a reaction of an acid (HNO_3) with a base (KOH) to produce salt (KNO_3) and water (H_2O) as products.

15. **2** *Note* the following oxidation number changes of Al and Cu^{2+}.

Al ---------> Al^{3+} + 3e- (each Al loses 3 e-)

Cu^{2+} + 2e- -----> Cu (each Cu^{2+} gains 2 e-)

Day 25: Answers and Explanations

16. **1** *Use* Table T percent composition equation to setup:

$$\% Mg = \frac{\text{Total Mass of Mg}}{\text{Gram-formula mass}} \times 100$$

$$\% Mg = \frac{24}{184} \times 100 =$$

17. **4** *Recall:* The difference between the Potential Energy (PE) of the products and the Potential Energy of the reactants is **ΔH (heat of reaction)**

ΔH = PE of products – PE of reactants

18. **1** *Note:* Energy on the right (the product side) of the equation.
Recall: Equations with energy to the right means energy is released, and the reaction is exothermic.

19. **2** *Note:* In the symbol $^{27}_{13}Al$, there are

13 protons (equal to atomic # 13 for Al)
14 neutrons = mass # (27) - protons (13)

Day 25: Answers and Explanations

20. 4 *Note:* To answer correctly, you must determine the particle that is released as each isotope changes to another.

Recall the following changes that occur during natural transmutations (decays)

During **alpha decays:** ***mass number*** *always decreases by* ***4***
atomic number *always decreases by* ***2***

During **beta decays**: ***mass number*** *remains constant (same)*
atomic number *always increases* by ***1***

During **positron emissions:** ***mass number*** *remains constant*
atomic number *always decreases* by ***1***

Note the following changes shown in the diagram

Note: $^{238}_{92}U$ changing to $^{234}_{90}Th$ is an **alpha decay**

Note: $^{234}_{90}Th$ changing to $^{234}_{91}Pa$ is a **beta decay**

Note: $^{234}_{91}Pa$ changing to $^{234}_{92}U$ is also a **beta decay**

Tracking your progress

If you have completed Day 1, 3, 5, 7 and 9 multiple choice question sets, you can easily check your progress and improvements in this question category.

. Go to page 211

. Plot and graph the number of points you got correct on each of the days using the first graph on the page (the 10-point graph)

You hope to see an upward trend on the graph, which will indicates improvement and progress. If not, study more from your review packets and books.

Day 26: Constructed Response Questions
10 points Part B-2 and C Practice

Start: Answer all questions on this day before stopping.

Base your answers to 1 through 3 on the information below.

In a laboratory, 0.100 mole of colorless hydrogen iodide gas at room temperature is placed in a 1.00-liter flask. The flask is sealed and warmed, causing the HI(g) to start decomposing to H_2(g) and I_2(g). Then the temperature of the contents of the flask is kept constant. During this reaction, the contents of the flask change to a pale purple-colored mixture of HI(g), H_2(g), and I_2(g). When the color of the mixture in the flask stops changing, the concentration of I_2(g) is determine to be 0.013 mole per liter. The relationship between concentration and time for the reactant and products is shown in the graph below.

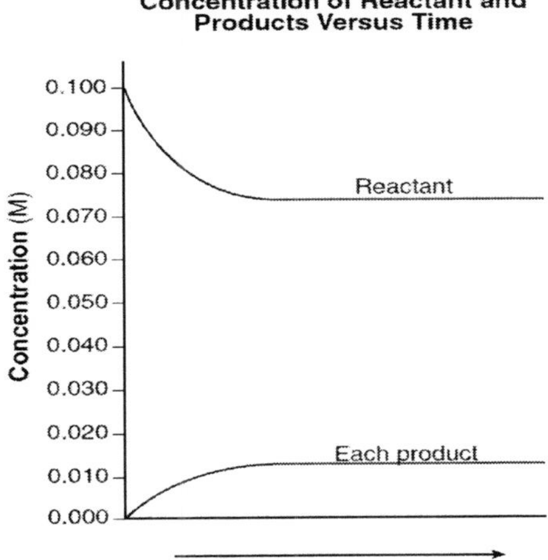

1. Write a balanced equation to represent the decomposition reaction occurring in the flask. [1]

Day 26: continue.

2. State, in terms of concentration, evidence that indicates the system in the flask has reached equilibrium. [1]

3. Calculate the mass of $I_2(g)$ in the flask at equilibrium. Your response must include both a correct numerical setup and the calculated result. [2]

4. Explain, in terms of electronegativity, why P-Cl bond in a molecule of PCl_5 is more polar than a P-S bond in P_2S_5. [1]

5. Describe one appropriate laboratory test that can be used to determine the malleability of a solid sample of an element at room temperature. [1]

Day 26: continue.

Base your answers to questions 22 to 24 on the information below.

The hydrocarbon 2-methylpropane reacts with iodine as represented by the balanced equation below. At Standard pressure, the boiling point of 2-methylpropane is lower than the boiling point of 2-iodo-2-methylpropane.

```
        H                                   H
        |                                   |
     H—C—H                               H—C—H
     H  |  H                             H  |  H
     |  |  |                             |  |  |
  H—C—C—C—H   +   I—I   ——→   H—C—C—C—H   +   H—I
     |  |  |                             |  |  |
     H  H  H                             H  I  H

  2-methylpropane                  2-iodo-2-methylpropane
```

6. To which class of organic compound does this organic product belong? [1]

7. Explain, in terms of bonding, why the hydrocarbon 2-methylpropane is saturated. [1]

8. Explain the difference in the boiling points of 2-methylpropane and 2-iodo-2-methylpropane in terms of both molecular polarity and intermolecular forces. [2]

   Molecular polarity: [1]

   Intermolecular forces: [1]

Day 26

Stop. Correct your answers and note how many correct **Points**

Day 26: Answers and Explanations

1. 1 point — **2HI ------> H_2 + I_2**

   Note: information needed to write this equation is given in the second sentence of the passage. Once the equation is written, you then can balance it.

2. 1 point — Acceptable responses include, but are not limited to:

   The concentrations stay constant (same).

   Concentration doesn't change

   Recall: at equilibrium: **Concentration** of substances stays the **constant** (same)

   Rate of forward and reverse reactions are **equal**

3. 2 points

   Mass of I_2 = moles of I_2 x formula mass of I_2

   Mass of I_2 = **0.013** x **254** *Setup* **[1 point]**

   Mass of I_2 = **3.3 grams** *calculated result* **[1 point]**

   Note: Award 1 point for mass of I2 in grams that is consistent with your setup.

4. 1 point — Acceptable responses include, but are not limited to:

   *The **electronegativity difference in P-Cl bond is greater than the electronegativity difference in P-S bond.***

   Recall: electronegativity value (Table S) difference determine the degree of polarity in bonds…

   The ***Higher the difference***: the ***more polar***, the ***more ionic***, and the ***less covalent*** the bond

   The ***Lower the difference:*** the **less polar**, the **less ionic**, and the **more covalent** the bond

   Note: P – Cl bond has electronegativity difference of: **1.0**

   Cl P

   3.2 - 2.2 = **1.0**

   P – S bond has electronegativity difference of : **0.4**

   S P

   2.6 - 2.2 = **0.4**

Day 26: Answers and Explanations

5. 1 point — Acceptable responses include, but are not limited to:

Hit (or strike) the solid with a hammer to see if it flattens int a thin sheet.

Recall: Malleability describes how easily a solid can be flattened when struck.

6. 1 point — **Halide** or **organic halide**

Note: The product contains iodine (a halogen, Group 17)

7. 1 point — Acceptable responses include, but are not limited to:
The hydrocarbon 2-methylpropane is saturated because:
It contains all single bonds between the carbon atoms.

8. 2 points — **Molecular polarity (1 point)**
2-methylpropane has a lower boiling point than 2-iodo-2-methylpropane because it **is less polar.**

Intermolecular forces: (1 point)
2-methylpropane has a lower boiling point than 2-iodo-2-methylpropane because it **has weaker intermolecular forces.**

Tracking your progress

If you have completed Day 14, 16, 18, 20, 22, 24, and 26 constructed response question sets, then you are done with the the second half of question sets in this category. You can easily check your progress and improvements in this question category.

. Go to page 212

. Plot and graph the number of points you got correct on each of these days

You hope to see an upward trend on the graph, which indicates improvement and progress.

Day 27: Practice Regents Exam 1
Part A and B-1

Start: Answer all questions in Part A and B-1 before stopping

Part A: Answer all questions in this part

Directions (1 – 30): For each statement or question, write on the separate answer sheet the number of the word or expression that, of those given, best completes the statement or answer the question. Some questions may require the use of the Reference Tables for Physical Setting/Chemistry.

1 What is the total number of valence electrons in a calcium atom in the ground state?
(1) 8
(2) 2
(3) 18
(4) 20

2 Which subatomic particles are located in the nucleus of an He-4 atom?
(1) electrons and neutrons
(2) electrons and protons
(3) neutrons and protons
(4) neutrons, protons, and electrons

3 In the late 1800s, experiments using cathode ray tubes led to the discovery of the
(1) electron
(2) neutron
(3) positron
(4) proton

4 The atomic mass of titanium is 47.88 atomic mass units. This atomic mass represents the
(1) total mass of all the protons and neutrons in an atom of Ti
(2) total mass of all the protons, neutrons, and electrons in an atom of Ti
(3) weighted average mass of the most abundant isotope of Ti
(4) weighted average mass of all the naturally occurring isotopes of Ti

5 An atom of which element has the largest atomic radius?
(1) Fe
(2) Mg
(3) Si
(4) Zn

6 Which element requires the *least* amount of energy to remove the most loosely held electron from a gaseous atom in the ground state?
(1) bromine
(2) calcium
(3) sodium
(4) silver

Day 27: Practice Regents Exam 1

7 A balanced equation representing a chemical reaction can be written using
(1) chemical formulas and mass numbers
(2) chemical formulas and coefficients
(3) first ionization energies and mass numbers
(4) first ionization energies and coefficients

8 Every water molecule has two hydrogen atoms bonded to one oxygen atom. This fact supports the concept that elements in a compound are
(1) chemically combined in a fixed proportion
(2) chemically combined in proportions that vary
(3) physically mixed in a fixed proportion
(4) physically mixed in proportions that vary

9 The percent composition by mass of nitrogen in NH_4OH (gram formula mass = 35 grams/mole) is equal to

(1) $\frac{4}{35} \times 100$
(2) $\frac{14}{35} \times 100$
(3) $\frac{35}{14} \times 100$
(4) $\frac{35}{4} \times 100$

10 Which Group 15 element exists as diatomic molecules at STP?
(1) phosphorus
(2) nitrogen
(3) bismuth
(4) arsenic

11 What is the total number of electrons shared in a double covalent bond?
(1) 1
(2) 2
(3) 3
(4) 4

12 Given the balanced equation representing a reaction:

$$Br_2 + \text{energy} \longrightarrow Br + Br$$

Which statement describes the energy change and bonds in this reaction?
(1) Energy is released as bonds are broken.
(2) Energy is released as bonds are formed.
(3) Energy is absorbed as bonds are broken.
(4) Energy is absorbed as bonds are formed.

13 Which substance can *not* be broken down by a chemical change?
(1) methane
(2) propanal
(3) tungsten
(4) water

14 Object *A* at 40.°C and object *B* at 80.°C are placed in contact with each other. Which statement describes the heat flow between the objects?
(1) Heat flows from object *A* to object *B*.
(2) Heat flows from object *B* to object *A*.
(3) Heat flows in both directions between the objects.
(4) No heat flow occurs between the objects.

15 Which unit can be used to express the concentration of a solution?
(1) L/s
(2) J/g
(3) ppm
(4) kPa

16 Which formula represents a mixture?
(1) $C_6H_{12}O_6(\ell)$
(2) $C_6H_{12}O_6(s)$
(3) $LiCl(aq)$
(4) $LiCl(s)$

17 Which sample has particles with the *lowest* average kinetic energy?
(1) 1.0 g of I_2 at 50.°C
(2) 2.0 g of I_2 at 30.°C
(3) 7.0 g of I_2 at 40.°C
(4) 9.0 g of I_2 at 20.°C

18 Which gas sample at STP has the same total number of molecules as 2.0 liters of $CO_2(g)$ at STP?
(1) 5.0 L of $CO_2(g)$
(2) 2.0 L of $Cl_2(g)$
(3) 3.0 L of $H_2S(g)$
(4) 6.0 L of $He(g)$

19 Petroleum can be separated by distillation because the hydrocarbons in petroleum are
(1) elements with identical boiling points
(2) elements with different boiling points
(3) compounds with identical boiling points
(4) compounds with different boiling points

20 Which compound is insoluble in water?
(1) KOH
(2) NH_4Cl
(3) Na_3PO_4
(4) $PbSO_4$

21 A gas sample is at 25°C and 1.0 atmosphere. Which changes in temperature and pressure will cause this sample to behave more like an ideal gas?
(1) decreased temperature and increased pressure
(2) decreased temperature and decreased pressure
(3) increased temperature and increased pressure
(4) increased temperature and decreased pressure

22 The isotopes K-37 and K-42 have the same
(1) decay mode
(2) bright-line spectrum
(3) mass number for their atoms
(4) total number of neutrons in their atoms

23 Which element is present in all organic compounds?
(1) carbon
(2) hydrogen
(3) nitrogen
(4) oxygen

24 Each of four test tubes contains a different concentration of HCl(aq) at 25°C. A 1-gram cube of Zn is added to each test tube. In which test tube is the reaction occurring at the fastest rate?

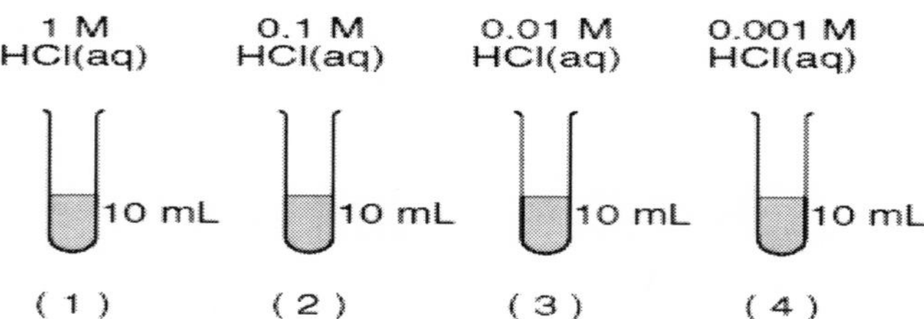

25 Which energy conversion occurs during the operation of an electrolytic cell?
(1) chemical energy to electrical energy
(2) electrical energy to chemical energy
(3) nuclear energy to electrical energy
(4) electrical energy to nuclear energy

26 Which compound is an Arrhenius acid?
(1) CaO
(2) HCl
(3) K_2O
(4) NH_3

Day 27: Practice Regents Exam 1

27 Based on the results of testing colorless solutions with indicators, which solution is most acidic?
(1) a solution in which bromthymol blue is blue
(2) a solution in which bromcresol green is blue
(3) a solution in which phenolphthalein is pink
(4) a solution in which methyl orange is red

28 According to one acid-base theory, water acts as an acid when an H_2O molecule
(1) accepts an H^+
(2) donates an H^+
(3) accepts an H^-
(4) donates an H^-

29 In which type of reaction is an atom of one element converted to an atom of a different element?
(1) decomposition
(2) neutralization
(3) saponification
(4) transmutation

30 Which nuclide is listed with its half-life and decay mode?
(1) K-37, 1.24 h, α
(2) N-16, 7.2 s, β−
(3) Rn-222, 1.6×10^3 y, α
(4) U-235, 7.1×10^8 y, β−

Day 27: Practice Regents Exam 1

Part B-1: Answer all questions in this part.

Directions (31 – 50): For each statement or question, write on the separate answer sheet the number of the word or expression that, of those given, best completes the statement or answer the question. Some questions may require the use of the Reference Tables for Physical Setting/Chemistry

31 The table below shows the number of subatomic particles in atom *X* and in atom *Z*.

Subatomic Particles in Two Atoms

Atom	Number of Protons	Number of Neutrons	Number of Electrons
X	6	6	6
Z	6	7	6

Atom *X* and atom *Z* are isotopes of the element
(1) aluminum (3) magnesium
(2) carbon (4) nitrogen

32 The greatest composition by mass in an atom of is due to the total mass of its
(1) electrons (3) positrons
(2) neutrons (4) protons

33 The bond between which two atoms is most polar?
(1) Br and Cl (3) I and Cl
(2) Br and F (4) I and F

34 In the formula $X_2(SO_4)_3$, the *X* represents a metal. This metal could be located on the Periodic Table in
(1) Group 1 (3) Group 13
(2) Group 2 (4) Group 14

35 At STP, which element is solid, brittle, and a poor conductor of electricity?
(1) Al (3) Ne
(2) K (4) S

36 Given the balanced equation representing a reaction:

$$2NaCl(\ell) \text{ --------- > } 2Na(\ell) + Cl_2(g)$$

A 1170.-gram sample of $NaCl(\ell)$ completely reacts, producing 460. grams of $Na(\ell)$. What is the total mass of $Cl_2(g)$ produced?

(1) 355 g
(2) 710. g
(3) 1420. g
(4) 1630. g

37 Given the formula representing a hydrocarbon:

```
H                   H   H
  \                 |   |
   C = C ---------- C - C - H
  /    |            |   |
H      |            H   H
   H - C - H
       |
       H
```

The molecular formula and the empirical formula for this hydrocarbon are

(1) C_5H_{10} and CH_2
(2) C_5H_{10} and CH_3
(3) C_4H_8 and CH_2
(4) C_4H_8 and CH_3

38 Which element forms an ionic compound when it reacts with lithium?

(1) K
(2) Fe
(3) Kr
(4) Br

39 Given the formula representing a molecule:

$$H - C \equiv C - H$$

The molecule is

(1) symmetrical and polar
(2) symmetrical and nonpolar
(3) asymmetrical and polar
(4) asymmetrical and nonpolar

40 Which compound has both ionic and covalent bonds?
(1) CO_2
(2) CH_3OH
(3) NaI
(4) Na_2CO_3

41 A cylinder with a movable piston contains a sample of gas having a volume of 6.0 liters at 293 K and 1.0 atmosphere. What is the volume of the sample after the gas is heated to 303 K, while the pressure is held at 1.0 atmosphere?
(1) 9.0 L
(2) 6.2 L
(3) 5.8 L
(4) 4.0 L

42 What is the minimum amount of heat required to completely melt 20.0 grams of ice at its melting point?
(1) 20.0 J
(2) 83.6 J
(3) 6680 J
(4) 45 200 J

43 As the temperature of a chemical reaction in the gas phase is increased, the rate of the reaction increases because
(1) fewer particle collisions occur
(2) more effective particle collisions occur
(3) the required activation energy increases
(4) the concentration of the reactants increases

44 The entropy of a sample of CO_2 increases as the CO_2 changes from
(1) gas to liquid
(2) gas to solid
(3) liquid to solid
(4) solid to gas

45 Which two factors must be equal when a chemical reaction reaches equilibrium?
(1) the concentration of the reactants and the concentration of the products
(2) the number of reactant particles and the number of product particles
(3) the rate of the forward reaction and the rate of the reverse reaction
(4) the mass of the reactants and the mass of the products

Day 27: Practice Regents Exam 1

46 Which formula represents an unsaturated hydrocarbon?

(1) C_5H_{12} (3) C_7H_{16}

(2) C_6H_{14} (4) C_8H_{14}

47 The reaction between an organic acid and an alcohol produces

(1) an aldehyde (3) an ether

(2) a ketone (4) an ester

48 Which balanced equation represents a redox reaction?

(1) $AgNO_3(aq) + NaCl(aq) \longrightarrow AgCl(s) + NaNO_3(aq)$

(2) $H_2CO_3(aq) \longrightarrow H_2O(\ell) + CO_2(g)$

(3) $NaOH(aq) + HCl(aq) \longrightarrow NaCl(aq) + H_2O(\ell)$

(4) $Mg(s) + 2HCl(aq) \longrightarrow MgCl_2(aq) + H_2(g)$

49 A solution with a pH of 2.0 has a hydronium ion concentration ten times greater than a solution with a pH of

(1) 1.0 (3) 3.0

(2) 0.20 (4) 20.

50 Which isotope is used to treat cancer?

(1) C-14 (3) Co-60

(2) U-238 (4) Pb-206

Day 27

Stop: Correct your answers and note how many correct **Points**

Day 27: Practice Regents Exam 1 Answers

Part A and B-1

1) **2**
2) **4**
3) **2**
4) **4**
5) **2**
6) **2**
7) **2**
8) **4**
9) **3**
10) **4**
11) **2**
12) **1**
13) **4**
14) **2**
15) **4**
16) **2**
17) **3**
18) **2**
19) **4**
20) **3**
21) **4**
22) **4**
23) **4**
24) **3**
25) **2**
26) **3**
27) **1**
28) **4**
29) **2**
30) **3**
31) **2**
32) **1**
33) **2**
34) **2**
35) **4**
36) **3**
37) **3**
38) **2**
39) **3**
40) **3**
41) **4**
42) **2**
43) **4**
44) **4**
45) **4**
46) **2**
47) **1**
48) **1**
49) **2**
50) **3**

Day 28: Practice Regents Exam 1
Part B-2 and C

Start: Answer all questions in Part B-2 and C before stopping.

Part B-2: Answer all questions in this part

Directions (51-63): Record your answers in the spaces provided in your Answer Booklet . Some questions may require the use of the Reference Tables for Physical Setting/Chemistry.

51 *In your answer booklet*, write an electron configuration for a silicon atom in an excited state. [1]

Base your answers to questions 52 and 53 on the information below.

Densities of Group 14 Elements

Element	Density at STP (g/cm^3)
C	3.51
Si	2.33
Ge	5.32
Sn	7.31
Pb	11.35

52 Identify *one* element from this table for *each* type of element: metal, metalloid, and nonmetal. [1]

53 Calculate the volume of a tin block that has a mass of 95.04 grams at STP. Your response must include *both* a numerical setup and the calculated result. [2]

Base your answers to questions 54 through 56 on the elements in Group 2 on the Periodic Table.

54. State the general trend in first ionization energy for the elements in Group 2 as these elements are considered in order from top to bottom in the group. [1]

55 State, in terms of the number of electron shells, why the radius of a strontium atom in the ground state is larger than the radius of a magnesium atom in the ground state. [1]

56 Explain, in terms of atomic structure, why the elements in Group 2 have similar chemical properties. [1]

Base your answers to questions 57 and 58 on the information below.

Heat is added to a sample of liquid water, starting at 80.°C, until the entire sample is a gas at 120.°C. This process, occurring at standard pressure, is represented by the balanced equation below.

$$H_2O(\ell) + \text{heat} \longrightarrow H_2O(g)$$

57 In the box *in your answer booklet*, using the key, draw a particle diagram to represent *at least five* molecules of the product of this physical change at 120.°C. [2]

58 On the diagram *in your answer booklet*, complete the heating curve for this physical change. [1]

Day 28: Practice Regents Exam 1

Base your answers to questions 59 and 60 on the information below.

In the gold foil experiment, a thin sheet of gold was bombarded with alpha particles. Almost all the alpha particles passed straight through the foil. Only a few alpha particles were deflected from their original paths.

59 State *one* conclusion about atomic structure based on the observation that almost all alpha particles passed straight through the foil. [1]

60 Explain, in terms of charged particles, why some of the alpha particles were deflected.

Base your answers to questions 61 through 63 on the information below.

Some Properties of Three Compounds at Standard Pressure

Compound	Boiling Point (°C)	Solubility in 100. Grams of H_2O at 20.°C (g)
ammonia	–33.2	56
methane	–161.5	0.002
hydrogen chloride	–84.9	72

61 Convert the boiling point of hydrogen chloride at standard pressure to kelvins. [1]

62 Explain, in terms of molecular polarity, why hydrogen chloride is more soluble than methane in water at 20.°C and standard pressure. [1]

63 Explain, in terms of intermolecular forces, why ammonia has a higher boiling point than the other compounds in the table. [1]

Day 28: Practice Regents Exam 1

Part C: Answer all questions in this part.

Directions (64-81): Record your answer in the spaces provided in your answer booklet. Some questions may require the use of the Reference Tables for Physical Setting/Chemistry.

Base your answers to questions 64 through 66 on the information below.

The diagram below represents an operating voltaic cell at 298 K and 1.0 atmosphere in a laboratory investigation. The reaction occurring in the cell is represented by the balanced ionic equation below.

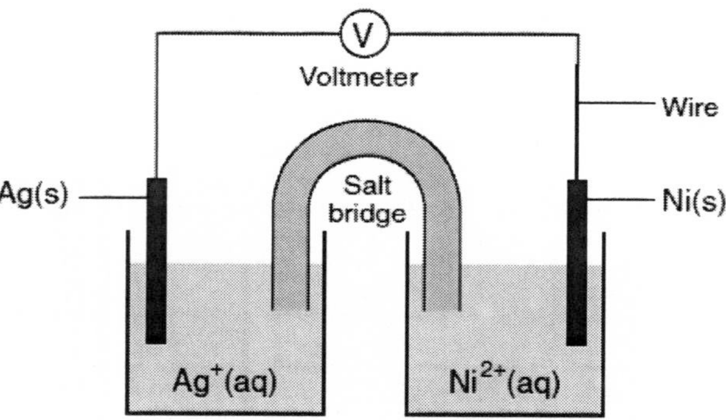

$$2Ag^{+}(aq) + Ni(s) \longrightarrow 2Ag(s) + Ni^{2+}(aq)$$

64 Identify the anode in this cell. [1]

65 Determine the total number of moles of Ni^{2+} (aq) ions produced when 4.0 moles of Ag^{+} (aq) ions completely react in this cell. [1]

66 Write a balanced half-reaction equation for the reduction that occurs in this cell. [1]

Base your answers to questions 67 through 69 on the information below.

Gasoline is a mixture composed primarily of hydrocarbons such as isooctane, which is also known as 2,2,4-trimethylpentane.

Gasoline is assigned a number called an octane rating. Gasoline with an octane rating of 87 performs the same as a mixture that consists of 87% isooctane and 13% heptane. An alternative fuel, E-85, can be used in some automobiles. This fuel is a mixture of 85% ethanol and 15% gasoline.

67 State the octane rating of a gasoline sample that performs the same as a mixture consisting of 92% isooctane and 8% heptane. [1]

68 In the space *in your answer booklet*, draw a structural formula for a molecule of 2,2,4-trimethylpentane. [1]

69 Identify the functional group in a molecule of ethanol in the alternative fuel E-85. [1]

Base your answers to questions 70 through 72 on the information below.

Hydrogen peroxide, H_2O_2, is a water-soluble compound. The concentration of an aqueous hydrogen peroxide solution that is 3% by mass H_2O_2 is used as an antiseptic. When the solution is poured on a small cut in the skin, H_2O_2 reacts according to the balanced equation below.

$$2H_2O_2 \longrightarrow 2H_2O + O_2$$

70 Identify the type of chemical reaction represented by the balanced equation. [1]

71 Calculate the total mass of H_2O_2 in 20.0 grams of an aqueous H_2O_2 solution that is used as an antiseptic.
Your response must include *both* a numerical setup and the calculated result. [2]

72 Determine the gram-formula mass of H_2O_2. [1]

Day 28: Practice Regents Exam 1

Base your answers to questions 73 and 74 on the information below.

The catalytic converter in an automobile changes harmful gases produced during fuel combustion to less harmful exhaust gases. In the catalytic converter, nitrogen dioxide reacts with carbon monoxide to produce nitrogen and carbon dioxide. In addition, some carbon monoxide reacts with oxygen, producing carbon dioxide in the converter. These reactions are represented by the balanced equations below.

Reaction 1: $2NO_2(g) + 4CO(g) \text{ -------- } > N_2(g) + 4CO_2(g) + 1198.4\text{ kJ}$

Reaction 2: $2CO(g) + O_2(g) \text{ ------- } > 2CO_2(g) + 566.0\text{ kJ}$

73 The potential energy diagram *in your answer booklet* represents reaction 1 without a catalyst. On the same diagram, draw a dashed line to indicate how potential energy changes when the reaction is catalyzed in the converter. [1]

74 Determine the oxidation number of carbon in *each* carbon compound in reaction 2.
Your response must include *both* the sign and value of *each* oxidation number. [1]

75 On the grid *in your answer booklet*, plot the data from the table. Circle and connect the points. [1]

Base your answers to questions 75 through 78 on the information below.

In one trial of an investigation, 50.0 milliliters of HCl(aq) of an unknown concentration is titrated with 0.10 M NaOH(aq). During the titration, the total volume of NaOH(aq) added and the corresponding pH value of the reaction mixture are measured and recorded in the table below.

Titration Data

Total Volume of NaOH(aq) Added (mL)	pH Value of Reaction Mixture
10.0	1.6
20.0	2.2
24.0	2.9
24.9	3.9
25.1	10.1
26.0	11.1
30.0	11.8

76 Determine the total volume of NaOH(aq) added when the reaction mixture has a pH value of 7.0. [1]

77 Write a balanced equation that represents this neutralization reaction. [1]

78 In another trial, 40.0 milliliters of HCl(aq) is completely neutralized by 20.0 milliliters of this 0.10 M NaOH(aq). Calculate the Molarity of the titrated acid in this trial. Your response must include *both* a numerical setup and the calculated result. [2]

Day 28: Practice Regents Exam 1

Base your answers to questions 79 through 81 on the information below.

The radioisotope uranium-238 occurs naturally in Earth's crust. The disintegration of this radioisotope is the first in a series of spontaneous decays. The sixth decay in this series produces the radioisotope radon-222. The decay of radon-222 produces the radioisotope polonium-218 that has a half life of 3.04 minutes. Eventually, the stable isotope lead-206 is produced by the alpha decay of an unstable nuclide.

79 Explain, in terms of electron configuration, why atoms of the radioisotope produced by the sixth decay in the U-238 disintegration series do not readily react to form compounds. [1]

80 Complete the nuclear equation *in your answer booklet* for the decay of the unstable nuclide that produces Pb-206, by writing a notation for the missing nuclide. [1]

81 Determine the original mass of a sample of Po-218, if 0.50 milligram of the sample remains unchanged after 12.16 minutes. [1]

Day 28

Stop: Correct your answers and note how many correct **Points**

Your Practice Regents Exam 1 Grade

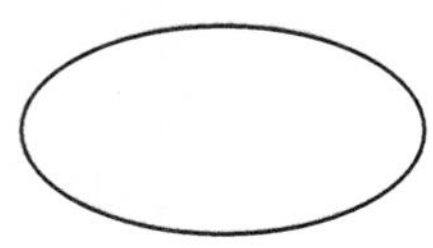

1. Your Raw Score: _____

Add your day 27 and day 28 points .

2. Your Regents Grade: _______

Use the conversion chart below. The Scale Score corresponding to your Raw Score is your Regents Grade for this exam.

Raw Score	Scale Score	Raw Score	Scale Score	Raw Score	Scale Score	Raw Score	Scale Score
85	100	63	74	41	59	19	39
84	98	62	73	40	58	18	38
83	96	61	72	39	58	17	36
82	94	60	71	38	57	16	35
81	93	59	71	37	56	15	33
80	91	58	70	36	55	14	32
79	90	57	69	35	55	13	30
78	88	56	69	34	54	12	29
77	87	55	68	33	53	11	27
76	86	54	67	32	52	10	25
75	85	53	67	31	52	9	23
74	84	52	66	30	51	8	21
73	83	51	66	29	50	7	19
72	82	50	65	28	49	6	17
71	81	49	64	27	48	5	14
70	80	48	64	26	47	4	12
69	79	47	63	25	46	3	9
68	78	46	62	24	45	2	6
67	77	45	62	23	44	1	3
66	76	44	61	22	43	0	0
65	75	43	60	21	41		
64	74	42	60	20	40		

Answer Booklet: Practice Exam 1

The University of the State of New York

RECENTS HIGH SCHOOL EXAMINATION

PHYSICAL SETTING CHEMISTRY

Part	Maximum Score	Student's Score
A	30	
B–1	20	
B–2	15	
C	20	

Total Written Test Score (Maximum Raw Score: 85) ☐

Final Score (from conversion chart) ☐

Student.. Sex: ☐ Male ☐ Female

Teacher..

School.. Grade ....

Answer all questions in this examination. Record your answers in this booklet.

Raters' Initials:

Rater 1 .... Rater 2 ....

Part A

1	11	21 ....
2	12	22 ....
3	13	23 ....
4	14	24 ....
5	15	25 ....
6	16	26 ....
7	17	27 ....
8	18	28 ....
9	19	29 ....
10	20	30 ....

Part A Score ☐

Part B–1

31	41 ....
32	42 ....
33	43 ....
34	44 ....
35	45 ....
36	46 ....
37	47 ....
38	48 ....
39	49 ....
40	50 ....

Part B–1 Score ☐

The declaration below must be signed when you have completed the examination.

I do hereby affirm, at the close of this examination, that I had no unlawful knowledge of the questions or answers prior to the examination and that I have neither given nor received assistance in answering any of the questions during the examination.

____

Signature

Answer Booklet: Practice Regents Exam 1

Part B–2	For Raters Only
51 ______________	51 ☐
52 Metal: ______________ Metalloid: ______________ Nonmetal: ______________	52 ☐
53 ______________ cm^3	53 ☐
54 ______________ ______________	54 ☐
55 ______________ ______________	55 ☐
56 ______________ ______________ ______________	56 ☐

Answer Booklet: Practice Regents Exam 1

For Raters Only

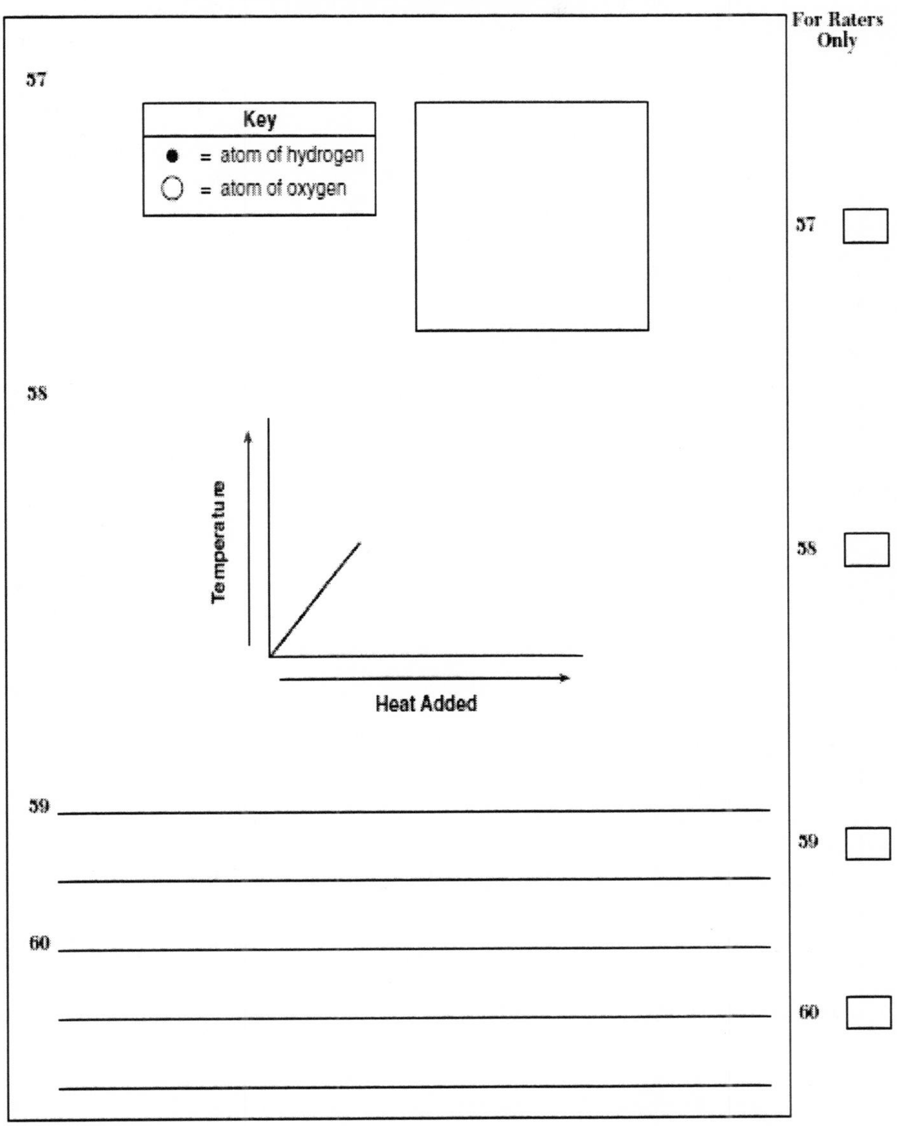

Answer Booklet: Practice Regents Exam 1

For Raters Only

61 ____________________ K

61 [ ]

62 ____

____

____

62 [ ]

63 ____

____

____

63 [ ]

[ ]

Total Score for Part B–2

Answer Booklet: Practice Regents Exam 1

Part C	For Raters Only
64 ________________	64
65 ________________ mol	65
66 ________________	66
67 ________________	67
68	68
69 ________________	69
70 ________________	70
71 ________________ g	71
72 ________________ g/mol	72

Answer Booklet: Practice Regents Exam 1

For Raters Only

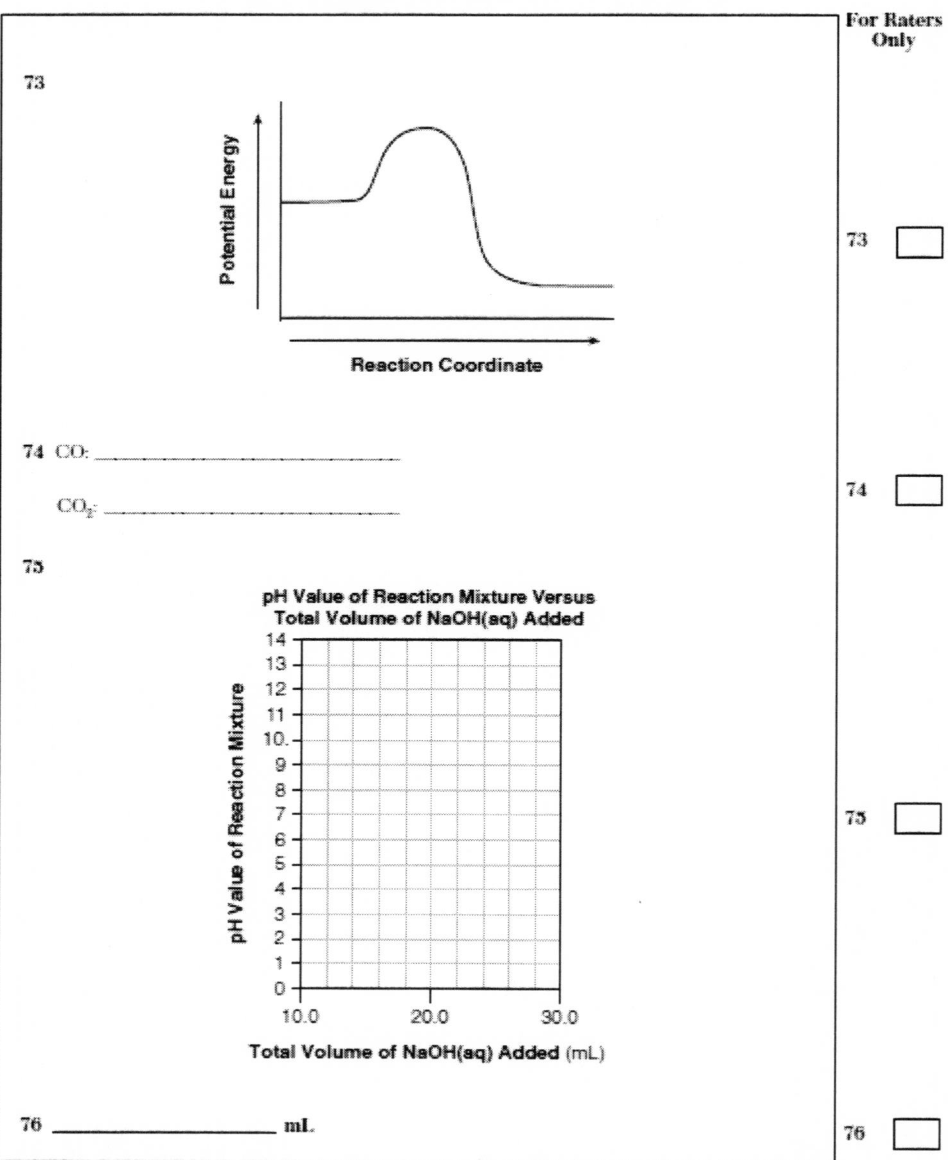

73 ☐

74 ☐

75 ☐

76 ____ mL

76 ☐

Answer Booklet: Practice Regents Exam 1

For Raters Only

77 ______________________ 77 [ ]

78

78 [ ]

______________ M

79 ______________________

______________________ 79 [ ]

____

80 ____________ → ${}^{4}_{2}He + {}^{206}_{82}Pb$ 80 [ ]

81 ______________ mg 81 [ ]

[ ]

Total Score for Part C

Day 28: Practice Regents Exam 1
Answers

Part B-2

Allow a total of 15 credits for this part. The student must answer all questions in this part.

51. 1 point — Acceptable responses include, but are not limited to:

2-7-5 *or* ***1-8-5*** *or* ***2-8-3-1***

52. 1 point — For a response indicating *one* metal, *one* metalloid, and *one* nonmetal.

Metal: tin *or* ***Sn*** *or* ***lead*** *or* ***Pb***

Metalloid: silicon *or* ***Si*** *or* ***germanium*** *or* ***Ge***

Nonmetal: carbon *or* ***C***

53. 2 points — Acceptable setups include, but are not limited to (**1 point**)

7.31 g/cm3 = $\frac{95.04}{V}$ or **$\frac{95.04}{7.31}$**

Acceptable calculated result (**1 point**)

13.0 cm³

or a **response consistent with your numerical setup.**

Significant figures do *not* need to be shown.

Note: Do *not* allow credit for a numerical setup and calculated result that are not related to the concept assessed by the question.

54. 1 point — Acceptable responses include, but are not limited to:

As atomic number increases, first ionization energy decreases.

First ionization energy decreases.

55. 1 point — Acceptable responses include, but are not limited to:

A strontium atom in the ground state has two more electron shells than a magnesium atom in the ground state.

An Mg atom has fewer electron shells.

Day 28: Practice Regents Exam 1
Answers

56. 1 point — Acceptable responses include, but are not limited to:

In the ground state, an atom of each element has two valence electrons.

The number of electrons in the outermost shell of each atom is the same.

57. 2 points — Allow a maximum of 2 points as follows:
Allow 1 point for ***at least five*** water molecules.
Allow 1 point for **all the particles drawn to represent the gas phase**.

Example of a 2-credit response:

Key
● = atom of hydrogen
○ = atom of oxygen

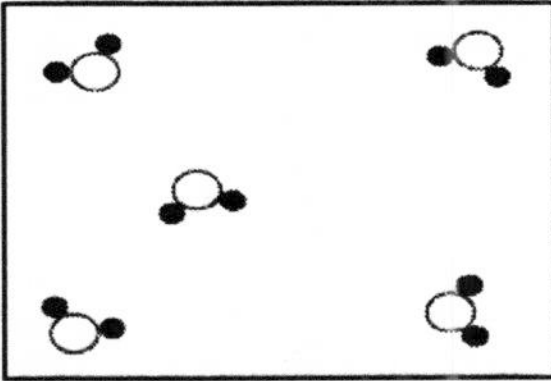

58. 1 point — Allow 1 point for drawing a line horizontally to represent **the phase change and extending the line with a positive slope to represent the gas phase,** only.

Example of a 1-credit response:

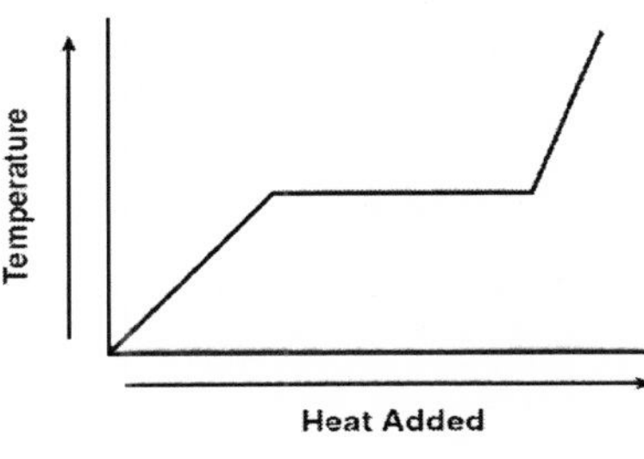

Day 28: Practice Regents Exam 1 Answers

59. 1 point — Acceptable responses include, but are not limited to:

Atoms are mostly empty space.

60. 1 point — Acceptable responses include, but are not limited to:

Alpha particles are positive and are repelled by the nucleus that is also positive.

Both protons and alpha particles are positively charged so they repel each other.

Protons and alpha particles have the same charge.

61. 1 point — **188 K.**

Significant figures do *not* need to be shown.

62. 1 point — Acceptable responses include, but are not limited to:

Molecules of CH_4 are nonpolar, but molecules of HCl and H_2O are both polar.

Hydrogen chloride and water are both polar.

63. 1 point — Acceptable responses include, but are not limited to:

Ammonia has stronger intermolecular forces than either methane or hydrogen chloride.

Ammonia has hydrogen bonding.

Day 28: Practice Regents Exam 1
Answers

Part C: Answers

Allow a total of 20 credits for this part. The student must answer all questions in this part.

64. 1 point — Acceptable responses include, but are not limited to:

Ni(s) the nickel electrode

Note: Do *not* allow credit for $Ni^{2+}(aq)$.

65. 1 point — ***2.0 mol.***

Significant figures do *not* need to be shown.

66. 1 point — Acceptable responses include, but are not limited to:

$Ag^{+} + e^{-} \longrightarrow Ag$

$2Ag^{+} + 2e^{-} \longrightarrow 2Ag$

67. 1 point — **92**

68. 1 point — Examples of 1-point drawing

```
        H       H
        |       |
      H-C-H   H-C-H
  H     |   H   |   H
  |     |   |   |   |
H-C-----C---C---C---C-H
  |     |   |   |   |
  H     |   H   H   H
      H-C-H
        |
        H
```

```
                 |
                -C-
   |   |   |    |   |
  -C---C---C----C---C-
   |   |   |    |   |
      -C-      -C-
       |        |
```

Day 28: Practice Regents Exam 1
Answers

69. 1 point — Acceptable responses include, but are not limited to:

-OH *or* ***alcohol*** *or* ***hydroxyl***

Note: Do *not* allow credit for hydroxide or OH-

70. 1 point — Acceptable responses include, but are not limited to:

decomposition

redox

71. 2 points — Acceptable setup includes, but are not limited to: (1point)

$$\mathbf{3 = \frac{x}{20.0\ g} \times 100} \quad \text{or} \quad \mathbf{(20)\ (0.03)}$$

Acceptable calculated result:

0.6 g

or for a response consistent with your numerical setup. Significant figures do *not* need to be shown.

Note: Do *not* allow credit for a numerical setup and calculated result that are not related to the concept assessed by the question

.

72. 1 point — **34 g/mol**.

Significant figures do *not* need to be shown.

Day 28: Practice Regents Exam 1 Answers

73. 1 point **Example of a 1-credit response:**

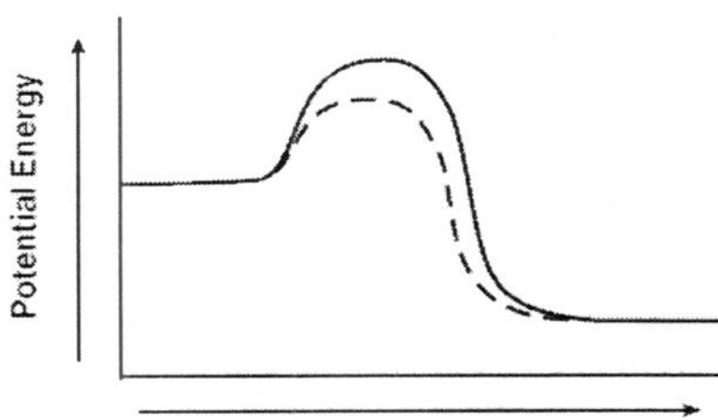

Note: Do *not* allow credit if the potential energy of the reactants or products is changed.

74. 1 point **+2** for carbon in CO and **+4** for carbon in CO_2.

75. 1 point **For correctly plotting all seven points ± 0.3 grid** space. Plotted points do *not* need to be circled or connected.

Example of a 1-credit response:

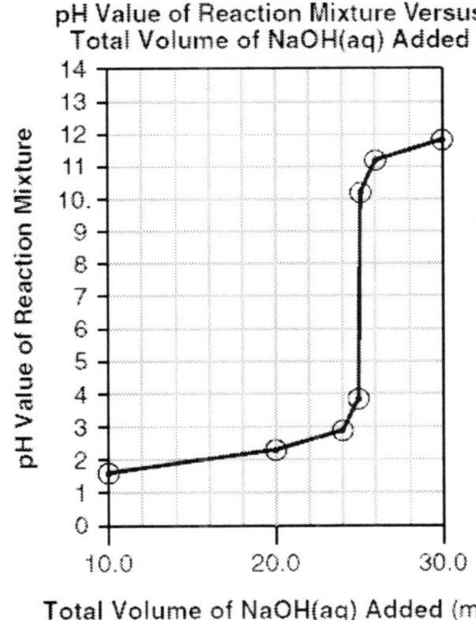

Day 28: Practice Regents Exam 1 Answers

76. 1 point **25.0 mL ± 0.6 mL**

or for a response consistent with your graph. Significant figures do *not* need to be shown.

77. 1 point Acceptable responses include, but are not limited to:

$NaOH(aq) + HCl(aq) \rightarrow NaCl(aq) + H_2O(\ell)$

$HCl + NaOH \rightarrow NaCl + H_2O$

$H^+(aq) + OH^-(aq) \rightarrow H_2O(\ell)$

$H_3O^+ + OH^- \rightarrow 2H_2O$

78. 2 points Acceptable setups includes, but are not limited to:

(*M*)(40.0 mL) = (0.10 M)(20.0 mL) *or* $\mathbf{\frac{(0.1)(20)}{40}}$

Acceptable calculated result:

0.050 M

or **for a response consistent with your setup**
Significant figures do *not* need to be shown.

Note: Do *not* allow credit for a numerical setup and calculated result that are not related to the concept assessed by the question.

79. 1 point Acceptable responses include, but are not limited to:

Radon-222 atoms have a complete outer shell of electrons and tend not to bond.

There are eight valence electrons in a radon atom.

Octet in valence shell

80. 1 point Acceptable responses include, but are not limited to:

Po-210 *or* $\mathbf{^{210}_{84}Po}$ *or* $\mathbf{^{210}Po}$

81. 1 point **8.00 mg.**

Significant figures do *not* need to be shown.

Day 29: Practice Regents Exam 2
Part A and B-1

Start: Answer all questions in Part A and B-1 before stopping.

Part A: Answer all questions in this part

Directions (1 – 30): For each statement or question, write on the separate answer sheet the number of the word or expression that, of those given, best completes the statement or answer the question. Some questions may require the use of the Reference tables for Physical setting/Chemistry.

1 A neutron has a charge of
(1) +1
(2) +2
(3) 0
(4) −1

2 Which particle has the *least* mass?
(1) alpha particle
(2) beta particle
(3) neutron
(4) proton

3 A sample of matter must be copper if
(1) each atom in the sample has 29 protons
(2) atoms in the sample react with oxygen
(3) the sample melts at 1768 K
(4) the sample can conduct electricity

4 In the electron cloud model of the atom, an orbital is defined as the most probable
(1) charge of an electron
(2) conductivity of an electron
(3) location of an electron
(4) mass of an electron

5 The elements on the Periodic Table are arranged in order of increasing
(1) atomic number
(2) mass number
(3) number of isotopes
(4) number of moles

6 Which element has the highest melting point?
(1) tantalum
(2) rhenium
(3) osmium
(4) hafnium

7 In a chemical reaction, there is conservation of
(1) energy, volume, and mass
(2) energy, volume, and charge
(3) mass, charge, and energy
(4) mass, charge, and volume

8 At STP, both diamond and graphite are solids composed of carbon atoms. These solids have
(1) the same crystal structure and the same properties
(2) the same crystal structure and different properties
(3) different crystal structures and the same properties
(4) different crystal structures and different properties

9 The gram-formula mass of a compound is 48 grams. The mass of 1.0 mole of this compound is
(1) 1.0 g
(2) 4.8 g
(3) 48 g
(4) 480 g

10 Given the balanced equation representing a reaction:

$$Cl_2 \text{ -------- } > Cl + Cl$$

What occurs during this reaction?
(1) A bond is broken as energy is absorbed.
(2) A bond is broken as energy is released.
(3) A bond is formed as energy is absorbed.
(4) A bond is formed as energy is released.

11 Which atom has the *weakest* attraction for the electrons in a bond with an H atom?
(1) Cl atom
(2) F atom
(3) O atom
(4) S atom

12 Which substance can *not* be broken down by a chemical change?
(1) ammonia
(2) mercury
(3) propane
(4) water

13 At standard pressure, how do the boiling point and the freezing point of NaCl(aq) compare to the boiling point and the freezing point of $H_2O(\ell)$?
(1) Both the boiling point and the freezing point of NaCl(aq) are lower.
(2) Both the boiling point and the freezing point of NaCl(aq) are higher.
(3) The boiling point of NaCl(aq) is lower, and the freezing point of NaCl(aq) is higher.
(4) The boiling point of NaCl(aq) is higher, and the freezing point of NaCl(aq) is lower.

14 The temperature of a sample of matter is a measure of the
(1) average kinetic energy of its particles
(2) average potential energy of its particles
(3) total kinetic energy of its particles
(4) total potential energy of its particles

Day 29: Practice Regents Exam 2

15 According to the kinetic molecular theory, the particles of an ideal gas
(1) have no potential energy
(2) have strong intermolecular forces
(3) are arranged in a regular, repeated geometric pattern
(4) are separated by great distances, compared to their size

16 Given the equation representing a closed system:

$$N_2O_4(g) \quad < \text{-------} > \quad 2NO_2(g)$$

Which statement describes this system at equilibrium?
(1) The volume of the $NO_2(g)$ is greater than the volume of the $N_2O_4(g)$.
(2) The volume of the $NO_2(g)$ is less than the volume of the $N_2O_4(g)$.
(3) The rate of the forward reaction and the rate of the reverse reaction are equal.
(4) The rate of the forward reaction and the rate of the reverse reaction are unequal.

17 In a chemical reaction, the difference between the potential energy of the products and the potential energy of the reactants is equal to the
(1) activation energy
(2) kinetic energy
(3) heat of reaction
(4) rate of reaction

18 For a given chemical reaction, the addition of a catalyst provides a different reaction pathway that
(1) decreases the reaction rate and has a higher activation energy
(2) decreases the reaction rate and has a lower activation energy
(3) increases the reaction rate and has a higher activation energy
(4) increases the reaction rate and has a lower activation energy

19 Which atoms can bond with each other to form chains, rings, or networks?
(1) carbon atoms
(2) hydrogen atoms
(3) oxygen atoms
(4) nitrogen atoms

20 A molecule of an unsaturated hydrocarbon must have
(1) at least one single carbon-carbon bond
(2) at least one multiple carbon-carbon bond
(3) two or more single carbon-carbon bonds
(4) two or more multiple carbon-carbon bonds

Day 29: Practice Regents Exam 2

21 Given a formula of a functional group:

```
    O
    ‖
 —C—OH
```

An organic compound that has this functional group is classified as

(1) an acid
(2) an aldehyde
(3) an ester
(4) a ketone

22 Which statement describes where the oxidation and reduction half-reactions occur in an operating electrochemical cell?

(1) Oxidation and reduction both occur at the anode.
(2) Oxidation and reduction both occur at the cathode.
(3) Oxidation occurs at the anode, and reduction occurs at the cathode.
(4) Oxidation occurs at the cathode, and reduction occurs at the anode.

23 Given a formula representing a compound:

```
     O   H   H   H
     ‖   |   |   |
 H — C — C — C — C — H
         |   |   |
         H   H   H
```

Which formula represents an isomer of this compound?

```
     H   H   H   O
     |   |   |   ‖
 H — C — C — C — C — H
     |   |   |
     H   H   H
```

(1)

```
     H   O   H   H
     |   ‖   |   |
 H — C — C — C — C — H
     |       |   |
     H       H   H
```

(2)

```
     H   H   H   O
     |   |   |   ‖
 H — C — C — C — C — OH
     |   |   |
     H   H   H
```

(3)

```
     H   H   O       H
     |   |   ‖       |
 H — C — C — C — O — C — H
     |   |           |
     H   H           H
```

(4)

24 Which energy conversion occurs in an operating electrolytic cell?
(1) chemical energy to electrical energy
(2) electrical energy to chemical energy
(3) nuclear energy to thermal energy
(4) thermal energy to nuclear energy

25 Which compounds can be classified as electrolytes?
(1) alcohols
(2) alkynes
(3) organic acids
(4) saturated hydrocarbons

26 Potassium hydroxide is classified as an Arrhenius base because KOH contains
(1) OH^- ions
(2) O_2^- ions
(3) K^+ ions
(4) H^+ ions

27 In which laboratory process is a volume of solution of known concentration used to determine the concentration of another solution?
(1) deposition
(2) distillation
(3) filtration
(4) titration

28 According to one acid-base theory, an acid is an
(1) H^+ acceptor
(2) H^+ donor
(3) OH^- acceptor
(4) OH^- donor

29 Energy is released during the fission of Pu-239 atoms as a result of the
(1) formation of covalent bonds
(2) formation of ionic bonds
(3) conversion of matter to energy
(4) conversion of energy to matter

30 Atoms of I-131 spontaneously decay when the
(1) stable nuclei emit alpha particles
(2) stable nuclei emit beta particles
(3) unstable nuclei emit alpha particles
(4) unstable nuclei emit beta particles

Day 29: Practice Regents Exam 2

Part B – 1: Answer all questions in this part.

Directions (31 – 50): For each statement or question, write on the separate answer sheet the number of the word or expression that, of those given, best completes the statement or answer the question. Some questions may require the use of the Reference Tables for Physical Setting/Chemistry.

31 Compared to the atoms of nonmetals in Period 3, the atoms of metals in Period 3 have
(1) fewer valence electrons
(2) more valence electrons
(3) fewer electron shells
(4) more electron shells

32 Which elements are malleable and good conductors of electricity?
(1) iodine and silver
(2) iodine and xenon
(3) tin and silver
(4) tin and xenon

33 Which atom in the ground state requires the *least* amount of energy to remove its valence electron?
(1) lithium atom
(2) potassium atom
(3) rubidium atom
(4) sodium atom

34 What is the chemical formula of iron(III) sulfide?
(1) FeS
(2) Fe_2S_3
(3) $FeSO_3$
(4) $Fe_2(SO_3)_3$

35 What is the percent composition by mass of sulfur in the compound $MgSO_4$ (gram-formula mass = 120. grams per mole)?
(1) 20.%
(2) 27%
(3) 46%
(4) 53%

36 Which compound becomes *less* soluble in water as the temperature of the solution is increased?
(1) HCl
(2) KCl
(3) $NaCl$
(4) NH_4Cl

37 Given the balanced equation representing a reaction:

$$2H_2 \quad + \quad O_2 \quad \text{------} > \quad 2H_2O$$

What is the mass of H_2O produced when 10.0 grams of H_2 reacts completely with 80.0 grams of O_2?
(1) 70.0 g
(2) 90.0 g
(3) 180. g
(4) 800. g

38 Given two formulas representing the same compound:

Formula A	Formula B
CH_3	C_2H_6

Which statement describes these formulas?
(1) Formulas *A* and *B* are both empirical.
(2) Formulas *A* and *B* are both molecular.
(3) Formula *A* is empirical, and formula *B* is molecular.
(4) Formula *A* is molecular, and formula *B* is empirical.

39 Given the balanced equation representing a reaction:

$$Zn(s) + H_2SO_4(aq) \text{------} > ZnSO_4(aq) + H_2(g)$$

Which type of reaction is represented by this equation?
(1) decomposition
(2) double replacement
(3) single replacement
(4) synthesis

40 In a laboratory where the air temperature is 22°C, a steel cylinder at 100.°C is submerged in a sample of water at 40.°C. In this system, heat flows from
(1) both the air and the water to the cylinder
(2) both the cylinder and the air to the water
(3) the air to the water and from the water to the cylinder
(4) the cylinder to the water and from the water to the air

41 Which diagram represents a physical change, only?

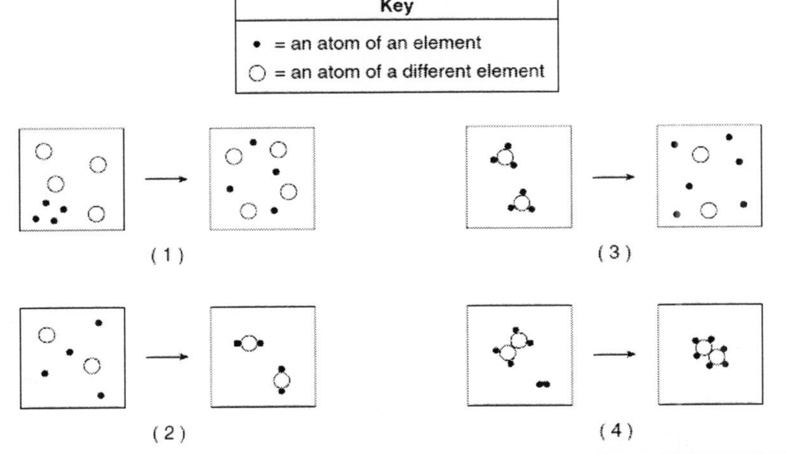

Day 29: Practice Regents Exam 2

42 During a laboratory activity to investigate reaction rate, a student reacts 1.0-gram samples of solid zinc with 10.0-milliliter samples of HCl(aq). The table below shows information about the variables in five experiments the student performed.

Reaction of Zn(s) with HCl(aq)

Experiment	Description of Zinc Sample	HCl(aq) Concentration (M)	Temperature (K)
1	lumps	0.10	270.
2	powder	0.10	270.
3	lumps	0.10	290.
4	lumps	1.0	290.
5	powder	1.0	280.

Which two experiments can be used to investigate the effect of the concentration of HCl(aq) on the reaction rate?

(1) 1 and 3
(2) 1 and 5
(3) 4 and 2
(4) 4 and 3

43 Which temperature change would cause a sample of an ideal gas to double in volume while the pressure is held constant?

(1) from 400. K to 200. K
(2) from 200. K to 400. K
(3) from 400.°C to 200.°C
(4) from 200.°C to 400.°C

44 A 36-gram sample of water has an initial temperature of 22°C. After the sample absorbs 1200 joules of heat energy, the final temperature of the sample is

(1) 8.0°C
(2) 14°C
(3) 30.°C
(4) 55°C

45 Which statement explains why Br_2 is a liquid at STP and I_2 is a solid at STP?

(1) Molecules of Br_2 are polar, and molecules of I_2 are nonpolar.
(2) Molecules of I_2 are polar, and molecules of Br_2 are nonpolar.
(3) Molecules of Br_2 have stronger intermolecular forces than molecules of I_2.
(4) Molecules of I_2 have stronger intermolecular forces than molecules of Br_2.

Day 29: Practice Regents Exam 2

46 Which balanced equation represents an oxidation-reduction reaction?

(1) $Ba(NO_3)_2$ + Na_2SO_4 -----> $BaSO_4$ + $2NaNO_3$
(2) H_3PO_4 + 3KOH -----> K_3PO_4 + $3H_2O$
(3) Fe(s) + S(s) --------> FeS(s)
(4) $NH_3(g)$ + HCl(g) ------> $NH_4Cl(s)$

47 Which solution reacts with LiOH(aq) to produce a salt and water?

(1) KCl(aq)
(2) CaO(aq)
(3) NaOH(aq)
(4) $H_2SO_4(aq)$

48 Which volume of 2.0 M NaOH(aq) is needed to completely neutralize 24 milliliters of 1.0 M HCl(aq)?

(1) 6.0 mL
(2) 12 mL
(3) 24 mL
(4) 48 mL

49 Which type of reaction releases the greatest amount of energy per mole of reactant?

(1) combustion
(2) decomposition
(3) nuclear fusion
(4) oxidation-reduction

50 Which balanced equation represents natural transmutation?

(1) ${}^{9}_{4}Be + {}^{1}_{1}H \rightarrow {}^{6}_{3}Li + {}^{4}_{2}He$
(2) ${}^{14}_{7}N + {}^{4}_{2}He \rightarrow {}^{17}_{8}O + {}^{1}_{1}H$
(3) ${}^{239}_{94}Pu + {}^{1}_{0}n \rightarrow {}^{144}_{58}Ce + {}^{94}_{36}Kr + 2{}^{1}_{0}n$
(4) ${}^{238}_{92}U \rightarrow {}^{234}_{90}Th + {}^{4}_{2}He$

Day 29

Stop: Correct your answers and note how many correct **Points**

Day 29: Practice Regents Exam 2 Answers

Part A and B-1

1) **3**
2) **2**
3) **1**
4) **3**
5) **1**
6) **2**
7) **3**
8) **4**
9) **3**
10) **1**
11) **4**
12) **2**
13) **4**
14) **1**
15) **4**
16) **3**
17) **3**
18) **4**
19) **1**
20) **2**
21) **1**
22) **3**
23) **2**
24) **2**
25) **3**
26) **1**
27) **4**
28) **2**
29) **3**
30) **4**
31) **1**
32) **3**
33) **3**
34) **2**
35) **2**
36) **1**
37) **2**
38) **3**
39) **3**
40) **4**
41) **1**
42) **4**
43) **2**
44) **3**
45) **4**
46) **3**
47) **4**
48) **2**
49) **3**
50) **4**

Day 30: Practice Regents Exam 2
Part B-2 and C

Start: Answer all questions in Part B-2 and C before stopping.

Part B-2: Answer all questions in this part

Directions (51-65): Record your answers in the spaces provided in your answer booklet. Some questions may require the use of the Reference Tables for Physical Setting/Chemistry.

51 Explain, in terms of protons and neutrons, why U-235 and U-238 are different isotopes of uranium. [1]

Base your answers to questions 52 through 54 on the information below.

The bright-line spectra for three elements and a mixture of elements are shown below.

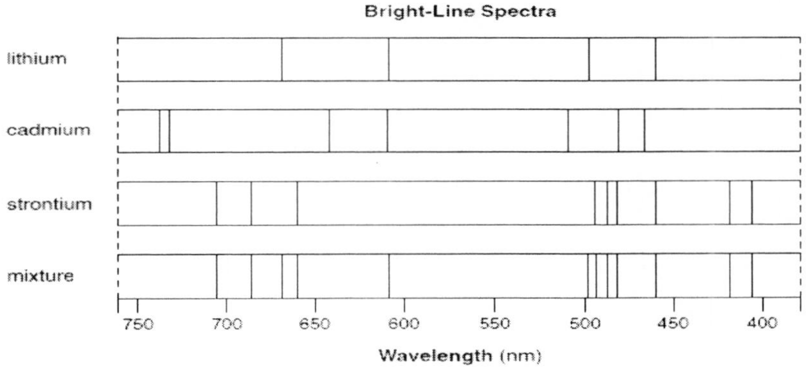

52 Explain, in terms of *both* electrons and energy, how the bright-line spectrum of an element is produced. [1]

53 Identify *all* the elements in the mixture. [1]

54 State the total number of valence electrons in a cadmium atom in the ground state. [1]

Day 30: Practice Regents Exam 2

Base your answers to questions 55 through 59 on the information below.

The ionic radii of some Group 2 elements are given in the table below.

Ionic Radii of Some Group 2 Elements

Symbol	Atomic Number	Ionic Radius (pm)
Be	4	44
Mg	12	66
Ca	20	99
Ba	56	134

55 On the grid *in your answer booklet*, mark an appropriate scale on the axis labeled "Ionic Radius (pm)." [1]

56 On the same grid, plot the data from the data table. Circle and connect the points. [1]

57 Estimate the ionic radius of strontium. [1]

58 State the trend in ionic radius as the elements in Group 2 are considered in order of increasing atomic number. [1]

59 Explain, in terms of electrons, why the ionic radius of a Group 2 element is smaller than its atomic radius. [1]

Base your answers to questions 60 and 61 on the information below.

The balanced equation below represents the decomposition of potassium chlorate.

$$2KClO_3(s) \rightarrow 2KCl(s) + 3O_2(g)$$

60 Determine the oxidation number of chlorine in the reactant in the equation. [1]

61 State why the entropy of the reactant is less than the entropy of the products. [1]

Day 30: Practice Regents Exam 2

Base your answers to questions 62 and 63 on the information below.

At 550°C, 1.00 mole of $CO_2(g)$ and 1.00 mole of $H_2(g)$ are placed in a 1.00-liter reaction vessel. The substances react to form $CO(g)$ and $H_2O(g)$. Changes in the concentrations of the reactants and the concentrations of the products are shown in the graph below

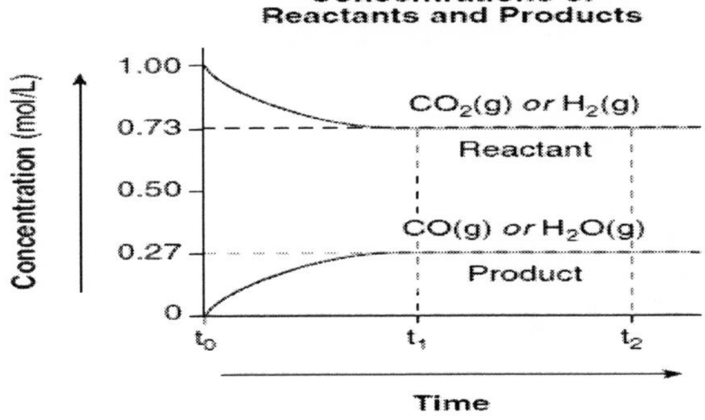

62 Determine the change in the concentration of $CO_2(g)$ between time t_0 and time t_1. [1]

63 What can be concluded from the graph about the concentrations of the reactants and the concentrations of the products between time t_1 and time t_2? [1]

Base your answers to questions 64 and 65 on the information below.

A reaction between bromine and a hydrocarbon is represented by the balanced equation below.

```
             H   H                      H   H   H
             |   |                      |   |   |
Br2 + H - C = C - C - H    --->    H - C - C - C - H
          |       |                     |   |   |
          H       H                     Br  Br  H
```

64 Identify the type of organic reaction. [1]

65 Write the name of the homologous series to which the hydrocarbon belongs. [1]

Day 30: Practice Regents Exam 2

Part C: **Answer all questions in this part.**

Directions (66-85): Record your answer in the spaces provided in your answer booklet. Some questions may require the use of the Reference Tables for Physical Setting/Chemistry.

Base your answers to questions 66 through 68 on the information below.

Ozone, $O_3(g)$, is produced from oxygen, $O_2(g)$, by electrical discharge during thunderstorms. The unbalanced equation below represents the reaction that forms ozone.

$$O_2(g) \text{ -------- > } O_3(g)$$

66 Balance the equation *in your answer booklet* for the production of ozone, using the smallest whole-number coefficients. [1]

67 Identify the type of bonding between the atoms in an oxygen molecule. [1]

68 Explain, in terms of electron configuration, why an oxygen molecule is more stable than an oxygen atom. [1]

Base your answers to questions 69 and 70 on the information below.

Natural gas is a mixture that includes butane, ethane, methane, and propane. Differences in boiling points can be used to separate the components of natural gas. The boiling points at standard pressure for these components are listed in the table below.

Data Table

Component of Natural Gas	Boiling Point at Standard Pressure (°C)
butane	−0.5
ethane	−88.6
methane	−161.6
propane	−42.1

69 Identify a process used to separate the components of natural gas. [1]

70 List the *four* components of natural gas in order of increasing strength of intermolecular forces. [1]

Day 30: Practice Regents Exam 2

Base your answers to questions 71 through 73 on the information below.

In 1864, the Solvay process was developed to make soda ash. One step in the process is represented by the balanced equation below.

$$NaCl + NH_3 + CO_2 + H_2O \rightarrow NaHCO_3 + NH_4Cl$$

71 Write the chemical formula for *one* compound in the equation that contains *both* ionic bonds and covalent bonds. [1]

72 Explain, in terms of electronegativity difference, why the bond between hydrogen and oxygen in a water molecule is more polar than the bond between hydrogen and nitrogen in an ammonia molecule. [1]

73 In the space *in your answer booklet*, draw a Lewis electron-dot diagram for the reactant containing nitrogen in the equation. [1]

Base your answers to questions 74 through 76 on the information below.

A student prepared two mixtures, each in a labeled beaker. Enough water at 20.°C was used to make 100 milliliters of each mixture.

Information about Two Mixtures at 20.°C

	Mixture 1	Mixture 2
Composition	NaCl in H_2O	Fe filings in H_2O
Student Observations	• colorless liquid • no visible solid on bottom of beaker	• colorless liquid • black solid on bottom of beaker
Other Data	• mass of NaCl(s) dissolved = 2.9 g	• mass of Fe(s) = 15.9 g • density of Fe(s) = 7.87 g/cm^3

74 Classify *each* mixture using the term "homogeneous" or the term "heterogeneous." [1]

75 Determine the volume of the Fe filings used to produce mixture 2. [1]

76 Describe a procedure to physically remove the water from mixture 1. [1]

Base your answers to questions 77 through 79 on the information below.

A student performed a laboratory activity to observe the reaction between aluminum foil and an aqueous copper(II) chloride solution. The reaction is represented by the balanced equation below.

$$2Al(s) + 3CuCl_2(aq) \rightarrow 3Cu(s) + 2AlCl_3(aq) + \text{energy}$$

Procedure	Observation
In a beaker, completely dissolve 5.00 g of $CuCl_2$ in 80.0 mL of H_2O.	• The solution is blue green.
Cut 1.5 g of Al(s) foil into small pieces. Add all the foil to the mixture in the beaker. Stir the contents for 1 minute.	• The surface of Al(s) foil appears partially black. • The beaker feels warm to the touch.
Observe the beaker and contents after 10 minutes.	• The liquid in the beaker appears colorless. • A reddish-brown solid is seen at the bottom of the beaker. • Some pieces of Al(s) with a partially black coating remain in the beaker.

77 State *one* observation that indicates Cu^{2+} ions became Cu atoms. [1]

78 Describe *one* change in the procedure that would cause the reaction to occur at a faster rate. [1]

79 State *one* safety procedure the student should perform after completing the laboratory activity. [1]

Day 30: Practice Regents Exam 2

Base your answers to questions 80 through 82 on the information below.

Some carbonated beverages are made by forcing carbon dioxide gas into a beverage solution. When a bottle of one kind of carbonated beverage is first opened, the beverage has a pH value of 3.

80 State, in terms of the pH scale, why this beverage is classified as acidic. [1]

81 Using Table *M*, identify *one* indicator that is yellow in a solution that has the same pH value as this beverage. [1]

82 After the beverage bottle is left open for several hours, the hydronium ion concentration in the beverage solution decreases to $^{1}/_{1000}{}^{th}$ of the original concentration. Determine the new pH of the beverage solution. [1]

Base your answers to questions 83 through 85 on the information below.

Polonium-210 occurs naturally, but is scarce. Polonium-210 is primarily used in devices designed to eliminate static electricity in machinery. It is also used in brushes to remove dust from camera lenses.

Polonium-210 can be created in the laboratory by bombarding bismuth-209 with neutrons to create bismuth-210. The bismuth-210 undergoes beta decay to produce polonium-210. Polonium-210 has a half-life of 138 days and undergoes alpha decay.

83 State *one* beneficial use of Po-210. [1]

84 Complete the nuclear equation *in your answer booklet* for the decay of Po-210, by writing a notation for the missing product. [1]

85 Determine the total mass of an original 28.0-milligram sample of Po-210 that remains unchanged after 414 days. [1]

Day 30

Stop: Correct your answers and note how many correct **Points**

Your Practice Regents Exam 2 Grade

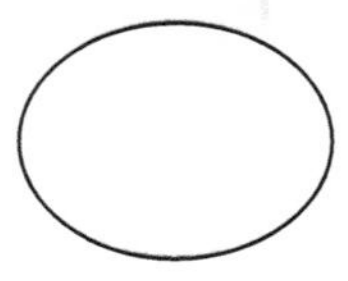

Determining your Practice Regents Exam 2 Grade

1. Your Raw Score: _____

Add your day 29 and day 30 points .

2. Your Regents Grade: _______

Use conversion chart below. The Scale Score corresponding to your Raw Score is your Regents Grade for this exam.

Raw Score	Scale Score	Raw Score	Scale Score	Raw Score	Scale Score	Raw Score	Scale Score
85	100	63	74	41	59	19	38
84	98	62	73	40	58	18	36
83	96	61	72	39	57	17	35
82	94	60	72	38	57	16	34
81	93	59	71	37	56	15	32
80	91	58	70	36	55	14	30
79	90	57	70	35	54	13	29
78	89	56	69	34	53	12	27
77	87	55	68	33	53	11	25
76	86	54	67	32	52	10	23
75	85	53	67	31	51	9	22
74	84	52	66	30	50	8	20
73	83	51	66	29	49	7	17
72	82	50	65	28	48	6	15
71	81	49	64	27	47	5	13
70	80	48	63	26	46	4	11
69	79	47	63	25	45	3	8
68	78	46	62	24	44	2	6
67	77	45	61	23	43	1	3
66	76	44	61	22	42	0	0
65	76	43	60	21	40		
64	75	42	59	20	39		

Answer Booklet: Practice Regents Exam 2

The University of the State of New York
REGENTS HIGH SCHOOL EXAMINATION

PHYSICAL SETTING CHEMISTRY

ANSWER BOOKLET

Student .... Sex: ☐ Male ☐ Female

Teacher ....

School .... Grade ....

Answer all questions in this examination. Record your answers in this booklet.

Part	Maximum Score	Student's Score
A	30	
B–1	20	
B–2	15	
C	20	

Total Written Test Score (Maximum Raw Score: 85) ☐

Final Score (from conversion chart) ☐

Raters' Initials:

Rater 1 .... Rater 2 ....

Part A

1 .... 11 .... 21 ....
2 .... 12 .... 22 ....
3 .... 13 .... 23 ....
4 .... 14 .... 24 ....
5 .... 15 .... 25 ....
6 .... 16 .... 26 ....
7 .... 17 .... 27 ....
8 .... 18 .... 28 ....
9 .... 19 .... 29 ....
10 .... 20 .... 30 ....

Part A Score ☐

Part B–1

31 .... 41 ....
32 .... 42 ....
33 .... 43 ....
34 .... 44 ....
35 .... 45 ....
36 .... 46 ....
37 .... 47 ....
38 .... 48 ....
39 .... 49 ....
40 .... 50 ....

Part B–1 Score ☐

The declaration below must be signed when you have completed the examination.

I do hereby affirm, at the close of this examination, that I had no unlawful knowledge of the questions or answers prior to the examination and that I have neither given nor received assistance in answering any of the questions during the examination.

____
Signature

Answer Booklet: Practice Regents Exam 2

Part B–2	For Raters Only	
51 ______________________		
______________________	51	
______________________		
52 ______________________		
______________________	52	
______________________		
53 ______________________	53	
54 __________	54	

Total Score for Part B–2

Answer Booklet: Practice Regents Exam 2

For Raters Only

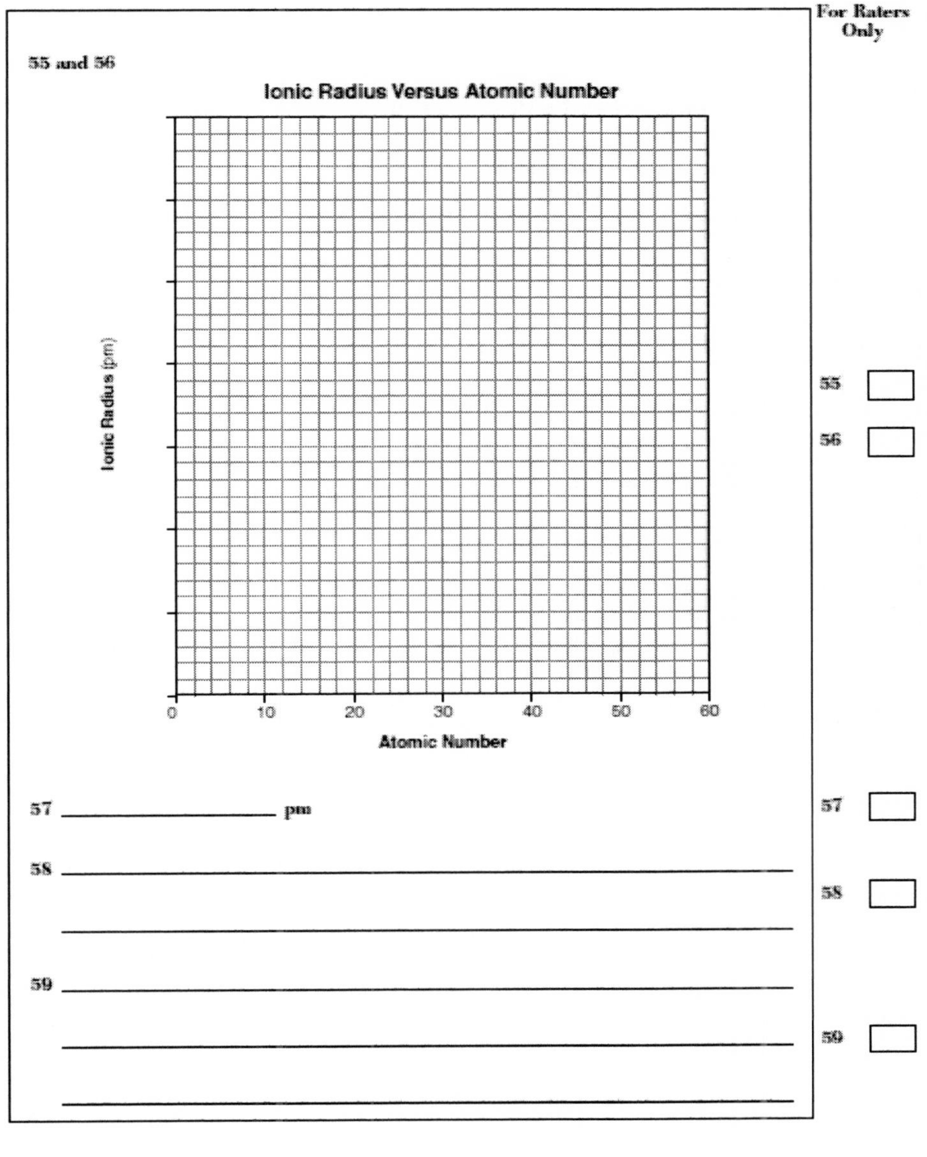

57 ______________ pm | 57 ☐

58 ______________ | 58 ☐

____

59 ______________

______________ | 59 ☐

____

Answer Booklet: Practice Regents Exam 2

	For Raters Only
60 ____________	60
61 ____ ____	61
62 ________________ mol/L	62
63 ____ ____	63
64 ________________________	64
65 ________________________	65
	Total Score for Part B–2

Answer Booklet: Practice Regents Exam 2

Part C

For Raters Only

66 ________ $O_2(g)$ $\xrightarrow{\text{electricity}}$ ________ $O_3(g)$ 66

67 ______________________ 67

68 ______________________

______________________ 68

____

69 ______________________ 69

70 ________ ________ ________ ________

Weakest intermolecular forces — Strongest intermolecular forces 70

71 ______________________ 71

72 ______________________

______________________ 72

____

73

73

Answer Booklet: Practice Regents Exam 2

For Raters Only

74 Mixture 1: ______________________ 74

Mixture 2: ______________________

75 ______________ cm^3 75

76 ______________________ 76

____

77 ______________________ 77

____

78 ______________________ 78

____

79 ______________________ 79

____

80 ______________________ 80

____

81 ______________________ 81

82 ________ 82

For Raters Only

83 ______________________ 83

____

84 $^{210}_{84}Po \rightarrow ^{4}_{2}He +$ ________ 84

85 ________ mg 85

Total Score

Day 30: Practice Regents Exam 2
Answers

Part B-2

Allow a total of 15 credits for this part. The student must answer all questions in this part.

51. 1 point — Acceptable responses include, but are not limited to:

A U-235 atom has 92 protons and 143 neutrons, and a U-238 atom has 92 protons and 146 neutrons.

A U-235 atom and a U-238 atom have the same number of protons but a different number of neutrons.

52. 1 point — Acceptable responses include, but are not limited to:

When electrons in an excited state return to a lower energy state, specific amounts of energy are emitted.

These energies are associated with specific wavelengths of light that are characteristic of the bright-line spectrum of an element.

Energy is emitted when excited electrons fall back to lower shells.

53. 1 point — ***lithium (Li)*** *and* ***strontium (Sr)***

54. 1 point — **2** *or* **two.**

Day 30: Practice Regents Exam 2

Answers

55. 1 point — ***For marking an appropriate scale.***
An appropriate scale is linear and allows a trend to be seen.

56. 1 point — ***For plotting all four points correctly ± 0.3*** **grid space.**
Plotted points do *not* need to be circled or connected.

Example of a 2-credit response for questions 55 and 56:

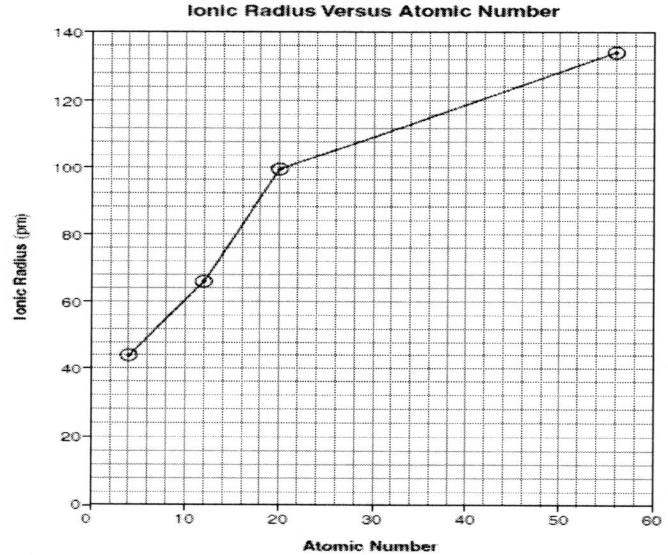

57. 1 point — ***117 pm*** *± 2 pm*

or for a **response consistent with your graph.**

58. 1 point — Acceptable responses include, but are not limited to:

As the atomic number of elements in Group 2 increases, the ionic radius increases.

The ionic radius increases.

Day 30: Practice Regents Exam 2
Answers

59.	1 point	Acceptable responses include, but are not limited to: ***The valence electron shell of a Group 2 atom is lost when it becomes an ion.*** ***A Group 2 ion has two fewer electrons than the atom from which it was formed.***
60.	1 point	***+5.***
61.	1 point	Acceptable responses include, but are not limited to: ***The gaseous product is more disordered than the solid reactant.*** ***The solid reactant is more ordered than the products.***
62.	1 point	Acceptable responses include, but are not limited to: ***−0.27 mol/L*** *or* ***0.27 mol/L***
63.	1 point	Acceptable responses include, but are not limited to: ***Between time t_1 and time t_2, the concentrations of the reactants and the concentrations of the products are no longer changing.*** ***The concentrations of the reactants and the products remain constant.*** ***The concentration of each reactant is 0.73 mol/L, and the concentration of each product is 0.27 mol/L.***
64.	1 point	Acceptable responses include, but are not limited to: **addition** *or* **halogenation** *or* **bromination**
65.	1 point	**alkene** *or* **alkenes.**

Day 30: Practice Regents Exam 2
Answers

Part C

Allow a total of 20 credits for this part. The student must answer all questions in this part.

66. 1 point   __**3**__ $O_2(g)$ ------------- > __**2**__ $O_3(g)$.

67. 1 point   Acceptable responses include, but are not limited to:

nonpolar covalent or **covalent** or **double covalent**

68. 1 point   Acceptable responses include, but are not limited to:

Both atoms in an O_2 molecule have achieved a noble gas electron configuration.

An oxygen atom does not have a stable octet of valence electrons.

69. 1 point   Acceptable responses include, but are not limited to:

fractional distillation *or* **distillation**

70. 1 point   Acceptable responses include, but are not limited to:

methane	***ethane***	***propane***	***butane***
Weakest intermolecular forces			Strongest intermolecular forces

or

CH_4	**C_2H_6**	**C_3H_8**	**C_4H_{10}**
Weakest intermolecular forces			Strongest intermolecular forces

Day 30: Practice Regents Exam 2
Answers

71\. 1 point **$NaHCO_3$** *or* **NH_4Cl.**

72\. 1 point Acceptable responses include, but are not limited to:

The electronegativity difference is 1.4 for H and O, which is higher than the 0.9 for H and N.

The difference in electronegativity between hydrogen and oxygen is greater than that for hydrogen and nitrogen.

73\. 1 point **Examples of 1-credit responses:**

```
  ••
H:N:H
  ••
  H

 H
 |
:N—H
 |
 H
```

74\. 1 point Acceptable *two* responses are:

Mixture 1: homogeneous

Mixture 2: heterogeneous

75\. 1 point **2.02 cm^3**.

Significant figures do *not* need to be shown.

76\. 1 point Acceptable responses include, but are not limited to:

Heat mixture 1 until all the water evaporates.

Allow the water to evaporate.

Day 30: Practice Regents Exam 2
Answers

77. 1 point Acceptable responses include, but are not limited to:

The solution is no longer blue green.

A reddish-brown solid is formed.

78. 1 point Acceptable responses include, but are not limited to:

Heat the solution before adding the aluminum foil.

Increase the concentration of the $CuCl_2$ solution.

Cut the Al foil into even smaller pieces.

79. 1 point Acceptable responses include, but are not limited to:

Thoroughly wash the lab equipment and return it to its proper storage place.

Dispose of the chemicals as directed by the teacher.

Wash hands before leaving the lab room.

80. 1 point Acceptable responses include, but are not limited to:

The beverage is acidic because its pH value is below 7.

A pH of 3 is in the acid range on the pH scale.

81. 1 point Acceptable responses include, but are not limited to:

bromthymol blue *or* ***bromcresol green*** *or* ***thymol blue***

82. 1 point **6** *or* **six.**

83. 1 point Acceptable responses include, but are not limited to:

Polonium-210 is used to eliminate static electricity in machinery.

Removes dust from camera lenses

84. 1 point Acceptable responses include, but are not limited to:

$^{206}_{82}Pb$ *or* **lead-206**

85. 1 point ***3.5 mg.***

Track Your Progress: Multiple Choice Questions

How well have you been improving on the multiple choice questions? It's easy to find out.

Get the correct points that you noted at the end of each multiple choice questions set (Odd Days).

Plot the points on the graph below. You hope to see an upward trend on each graph.

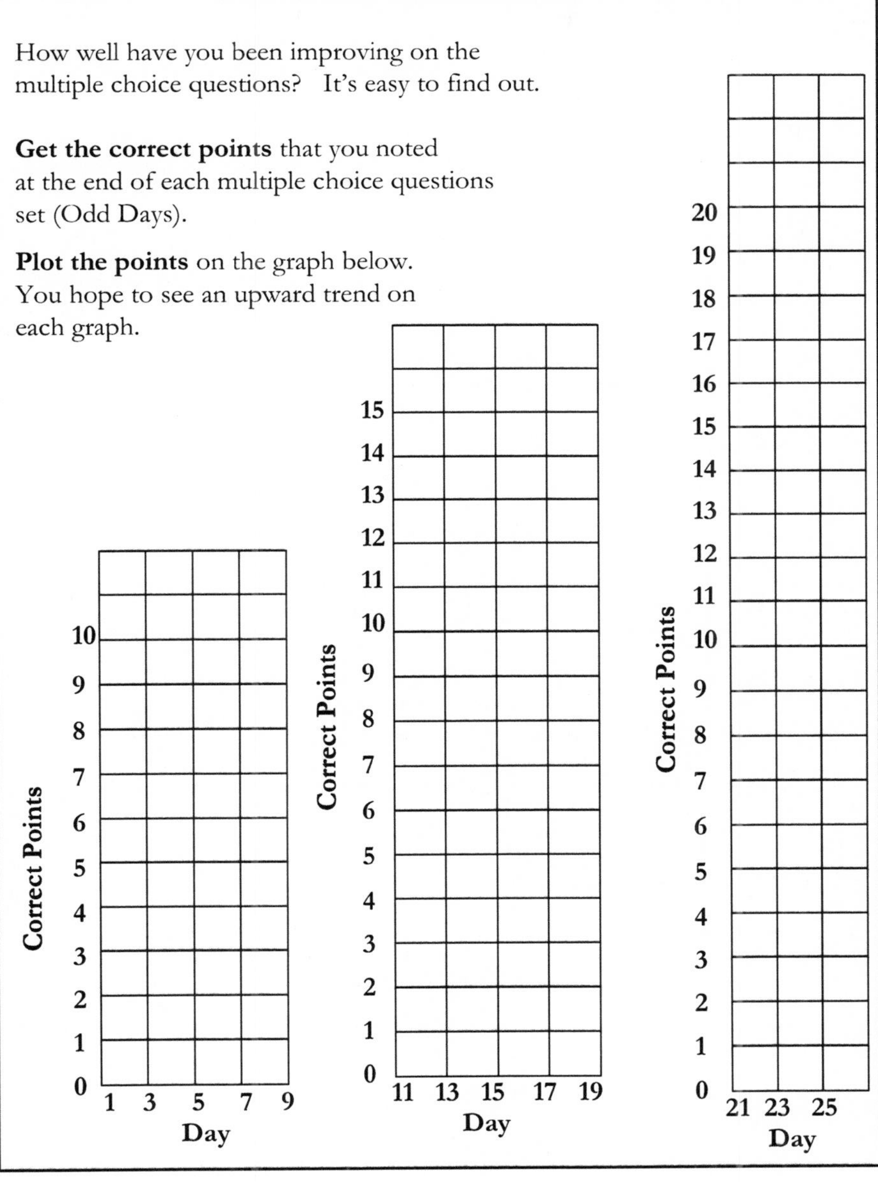

Track Your Progress: Constructed Response Questions

How well have you been improving on the constructed response questions? It's easy to find out.

Get the correct points that you noted at the end of each constructed response questions set (Even Days).

Plot the points on the graph below.
You hope to see an upward trend on the graph.

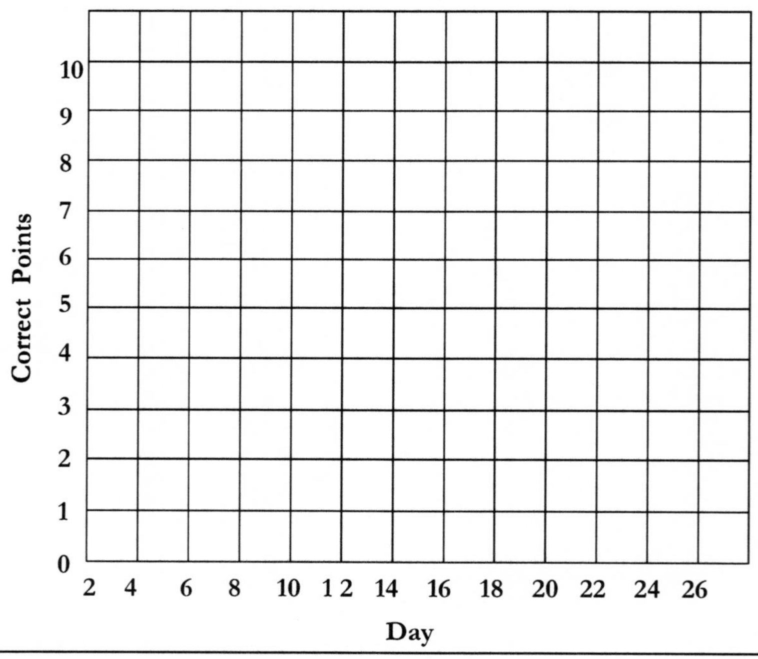

Reference Tables

Table A

Standard Temperature and Pressure

Name	Value	Unit
Standard Pressure	101.3 kPa 1 atm	kilopascal atmosphere
Standard Temperature	273 K 0°C	kelvin degree Celsius

Table B

Heat of Fusion	334 J/g
Heat of Vaporization	2260 J/g
Specific Heat Capacity of $H_2O(\ell)$	4.18 J/g•K

Table C

Selected Prefixes

Factor	Prefix	Symbol
10^{3}	kilo-	k
10^{-1}	deci-	d
10^{-2}	centi-	c
10^{-3}	milli-	m
10^{-6}	micro-	μ
10^{-9}	nano-	n
10^{-12}	pico-	p

Table D

Selected Units

Symbol	Name	Quantity
m	meter	length
g	gram	mass
Pa	pascal	pressure
K	kelvin	temperature
mol	mole	amount of substance
J	joule	energy, work, quantity of heat
s	second	time
min	minute	time
h	hour	time
d	day	time
y	year	time
L	liter	volume
ppm	parts per million	concentration
M	molarity	solution concentration
u	atomic mass unit	atomic mass

Table E

Selected Polyatomic Ions

Formula	Name
H_3O^+	hydronium
Hg_2^{2+}	mercury(I)
NH_4^+	ammonium
$C_2H_3O_2^-$ / CH_3COO^-	acetate
CN^-	cyanide
CO_3^{2-}	carbonate
HCO_3^-	hydrogen carbonate
$C_2O_4^{2-}$	oxalate
ClO^-	hypochlorite
ClO_2^-	chlorite
ClO_3^-	chlorate
ClO_4^-	perchlorate

Formula	Name
CrO_4^{2-}	chromate
$Cr_2O_7^{2-}$	dichromate
MnO_4^-	permanganate
NO_2^-	nitrite
NO_3^-	nitrate
O_2^{2-}	peroxide
OH^-	hydroxide
PO_4^{3-}	phosphate
SCN^-	thiocyanate
SO_3^{2-}	sulfite
SO_4^{2-}	sulfate
HSO_4^-	hydrogen sulfate
$S_2O_3^{2-}$	thiosulfate

Table F
Solubility Guidelines

Ions That Form *Soluble* Compounds	Exceptions
Group 1 ions (Li^+, Na^+, etc.)	
ammonium (NH_4^+)	
nitrate (NO_3^-)	
acetate ($C_2H_3O_2^-$ or CH_3COO^-)	
hydrogen carbonate (HCO_3^-)	
chlorate (ClO_3^-)	
halides (Cl^-, Br^-, I^-)	when combined with Ag^+, Pb^{2+}, or Hg_2^{2+}
sulfates (SO_4^{2-})	when combined with Ag^+, Ca^{2+}, Sr^{2+}, Ba^{2+}, or Pb^{2+}

Ions That Form *Insoluble* Compounds*	Exceptions
carbonate (CO_3^{2-})	when combined with Group 1 ions or ammonium (NH_4^+)
chromate (CrO_4^{2-})	when combined with Group 1 ions, Ca^{2+}, Mg^{2+}, or ammonium (NH_4^+)
phosphate (PO_4^{3-})	when combined with Group 1 ions or ammonium (NH_4^+)
sulfide (S^{2-})	when combined with Group 1 ions or ammonium (NH_4^+)
hydroxide (OH^-)	when combined with Group 1 ions, Ca^{2+}, Ba^{2+}, Sr^{2+}, or ammonium (NH_4^+)

*compounds having very low solubility in H_2O

Table G
Solubility Curves at Standard Pressure

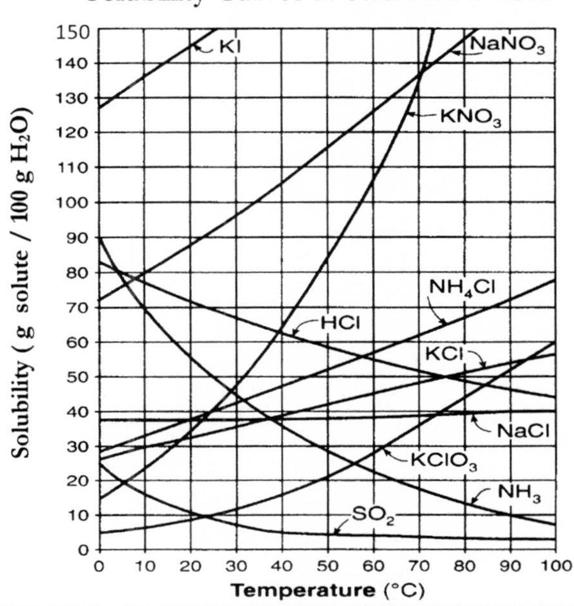

Table H

Vapor Pressure of Four Liquids

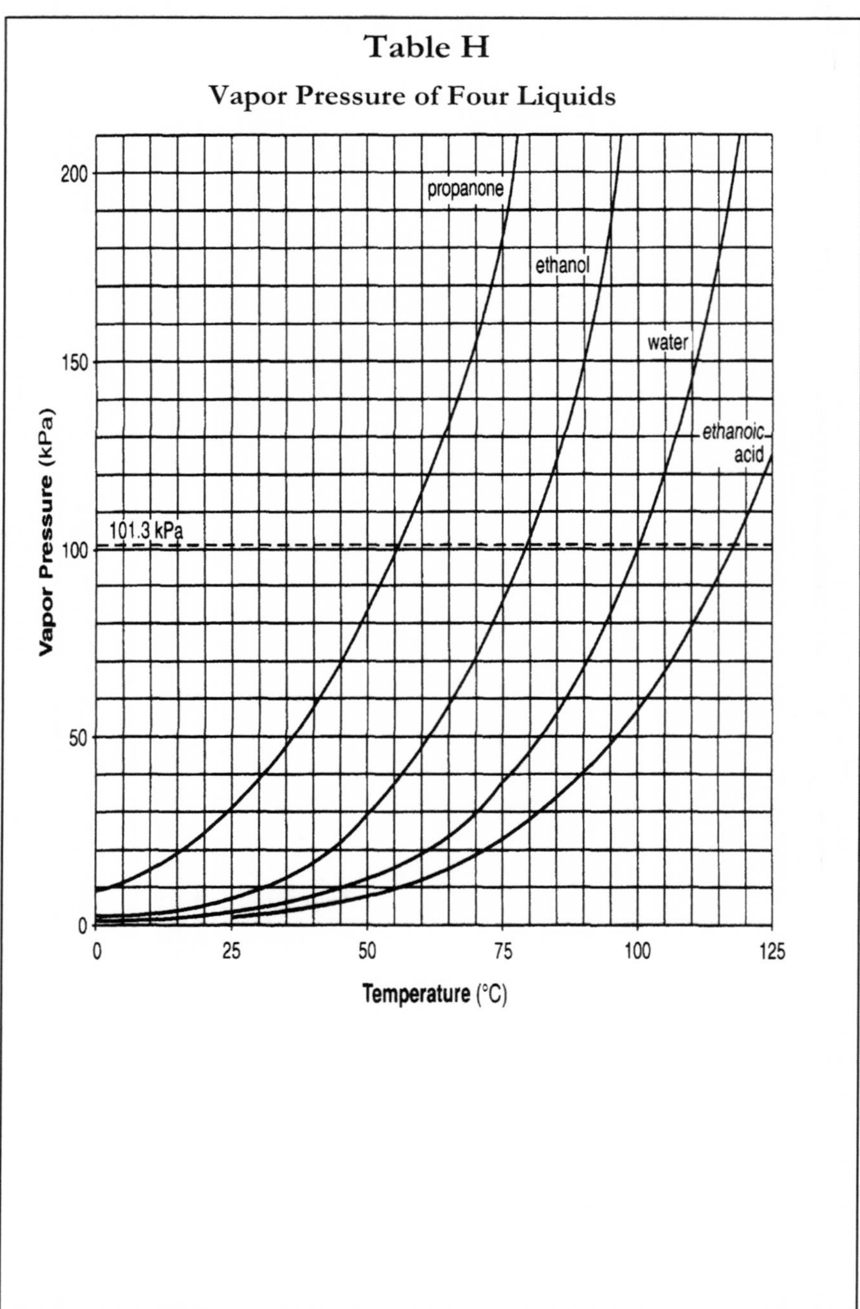

Table I
Heat of Reactions at 101.3 kPa and 298 K

Reaction	ΔH (kJ)*
$CH_4(g) + 2O_2(g) \longrightarrow CO_2(g) + 2H_2O(\ell)$	-890.4
$C_3H_8(g) + 5O_2(g) \longrightarrow 3CO_2(g) + 4H_2O(\ell)$	-2219.2
$2C_8H_{18}(\ell) + 25O_2(g) \longrightarrow 16CO_2(g) + 18H_2O(\ell)$	-10943
$2CH_3OH(\ell) + 3O_2(g) \longrightarrow 2CO_2(g) + 4H_2O(\ell)$	-1452
$C_2H_5OH(\ell) + 3O_2(g) \longrightarrow 2CO_2(g) + 3H_2O(\ell)$	-1367
$C_6H_{12}O_6(s) + 6O_2(g) \longrightarrow 6CO_2(g) + 6H_2O(\ell)$	-2804
$2CO(g) + O_2(g) \longrightarrow 2CO_2(g)$	-566.0
$C(s) + O_2(g) \longrightarrow CO_2(g)$	-393.5
$4Al(s) + 3O_2(g) \longrightarrow 2Al_2O_3(s)$	-3351
$N_2(g) + O_2(g) \longrightarrow 2NO(g)$	+182.6
$N_2(g) + 2O_2(g) \longrightarrow 2NO_2(g)$	+66.4
$2H_2(g) + O_2(g) \longrightarrow 2H_2O(g)$	-483.6
$2H_2(g) + O_2(g) \longrightarrow 2H_2O(\ell)$	-571.6
$N_2(g) + 3H_2(g) \longrightarrow 2NH_3(g)$	-91.8
$2C(s) + 3H_2(g) \longrightarrow C_2H_6(g)$	-84.0
$2C(s) + 2H_2(g) \longrightarrow C_2H_4(g)$	+52.4
$2C(s) + H_2(g) \longrightarrow C_2H_2(g)$	+227.4
$H_2(g) + I_2(g) \longrightarrow 2HI(g)$	+53.0
$KNO_3(s) \xrightarrow{H_2O} K^+(aq) + NO_3^-(aq)$	+34.89
$NaOH(s) \xrightarrow{H_2O} Na^+(aq) + OH^-(aq)$	-44.51
$NH_4Cl(s) \xrightarrow{H_2O} NH_4^+(aq) + Cl^-(aq)$	+14.78
$NH_4NO_3(s) \xrightarrow{H_2O} NH_4^+(aq) + NO_3^-(aq)$	+25.69
$NaCl(s) \xrightarrow{H_2O} Na^+(aq) + Cl^-(aq)$	+3.88
$LiBr(s) \xrightarrow{H_2O} Li^+(aq) + Br^-(aq)$	-48.83
$H^+(aq) + OH^-(aq) \longrightarrow H_2O(\ell)$	-55.8

*The ΔH values are based on molar quantities represented in the equations.

A minus sign indicates an exothermic reaction.

Table J
Activity Series

Most Active ↓ Least Active	Metals	Nonmetals	Most Active ↓ Least Active
	Li	F_2	
	Rb	Cl_2	
	K	Br_2	
	Cs	I_2	
	Ba		
	Sr		
	Ca		
	Na		
	Mg		
	Al		
	Ti		
	Mn		
	Zn		
	Cr		
	Fe		
	Co		
	Ni		
	Sn		
	Pb		
	H_2		
	Cu		
	Ag		
	Au		

Activity Series is based on the hydrogen standard.

H_2 is *not* a metal.

Table K
Common Acids

Formula	Name
$HCl(aq)$	hydrochloric acid
$HNO_2(aq)$	nitrous acid
$HNO_3(aq)$	nitric acid
$H_2SO_3(aq)$	sulfurous acid
$H_2SO_4(aq)$	sulfuric acid
$H_3PO_4(aq)$	phosphoric acid
$H_2CO_3(aq)$ or $CO_2(aq)$	carbonic acid
$CH_3COOH(aq)$ or $HC_2H_3O_2(aq)$	ethanoic acid (acetic acid)

Table L
Common Bases

Formula	Name
$NaOH(aq)$	sodium hydroxide
$KOH(aq)$	potassium hydroxide
$Ca(OH)_2(aq)$	calcium hydroxide
$NH_3(aq)$	aqueous ammonia

Table M
Common Acid-Base Indicators

Indicator	Approximate pH Range for Color Change	Color Change
methyl orange	3.1–4.4	red to yellow
bromthymol blue	6.0–7.6	yellow to blue
phenolphthalein	8–9	colorless to pink
litmus	4.5–8.3	red to blue
bromcresol green	3.8–5.4	yellow to blue
thymol blue	8.0–9.6	yellow to blue

Table N
Selected Radioisotopes

Nuclide	Half-Life	Decay Mode	Nuclide Name
^{198}Au	2.695 d	β^-	gold-198
^{14}C	5715 y	β^-	carbon-14
^{37}Ca	182 ms	β^+	calcium-37
^{60}Co	5.271 y	β^-	cobalt-60
^{137}Cs	30.2 y	β^-	cesium-137
^{53}Fe	8.51 min	β^+	iron-53
^{220}Fr	27.4 s	α	francium-220
^{3}H	12.31 y	β^-	hydrogen-3
^{131}I	8.021 d	β^-	iodine-131
^{37}K	1.23 s	β^+	potassium-37
^{42}K	12.36 h	β^-	potassium-42
^{85}Kr	10.73 y	β^-	krypton-85
^{16}N	7.13 s	β^-	nitrogen-16
^{19}Ne	17.22 s	β^+	neon-19
^{32}P	14.28 d	β^-	phosphorus-32
^{239}Pu	2.410×10^4 y	α	plutonium-239
^{226}Ra	1599 y	α	radium-226
^{222}Rn	3.823 d	α	radon-222
^{90}Sr	29.1 y	β^-	strontium-90
^{99}Tc	2.13×10^5 y	β^-	technetium-99
^{232}Th	1.40×10^{10} y	α	thorium-232
^{233}U	1.592×10^5 y	α	uranium-233
^{235}U	7.04×10^8 y	α	uranium-235
^{238}U	4.47×10^9 y	α	uranium-238

Table O
Symbols Used in Nuclear Chemistry

Name	Notation	Symbol
alpha particle	$^{4}_{2}He$ or $^{4}_{2}\alpha$	α
beta particle (electron)	$^{0}_{-1}e$ or $^{0}_{-1}\beta$	β^-
gamma radiation	$^{0}_{0}\gamma$	γ
neutron	$^{1}_{0}n$	n
proton	$^{1}_{1}H$ or $^{1}_{1}p$	p
positron	$^{0}_{+1}e$ or $^{0}_{+1}\beta$	β^+

Table P
Organic Prefixes

Prefix	Number of Carbon Atoms
meth-	1
eth-	2
prop-	3
but-	4
pent-	5
hex-	6
hept-	7
oct-	8
non-	9
dec-	10

Table Q
Homologous Series of Hydrocarbons

Name	General Formula	Examples	
		Name	Structural Formula
alkanes	C_nH_{2n+2}	ethane	H H / | | / H–C–C–H / | | / H H
alkenes	C_nH_{2n}	ethene	H H / \ / / C=C / / \ / H H
alkynes	C_nH_{2n-2}	ethyne	H–C≡C–H

Note: n = number of carbon atoms

H–C≡C–H

Table R
Organic Functional Groups

Class of Compound	Functional Group	General Formula	Example
halide (halocarbon)	—F (fluoro-) —Cl (chloro-) —Br (bromo-) —I (iodo-)	R—X (X represents any halogen)	$CH_3CHClCH_3$ 2-chloropropane
alcohol	—OH	R—OH	$CH_3CH_2CH_2OH$ 1-propanol
ether	—O—	R—O—R'	$CH_3OCH_2CH_3$ methyl ethyl ether
aldehyde	$-\overset{\overset{O}{\|\|}}{C}-H$	$R-\overset{\overset{O}{\|\|}}{C}-H$	$CH_3CH_2\overset{\overset{O}{\|\|}}{C}-H$ propanal
ketone	$-\overset{\overset{O}{\|\|}}{C}-$	$R-\overset{\overset{O}{\|\|}}{C}-R'$	$CH_3\overset{\overset{O}{\|\|}}{C}CH_2CH_2CH_3$ 2-pentanone
organic acid	$-\overset{\overset{O}{\|\|}}{C}-OH$	$R-\overset{\overset{O}{\|\|}}{C}-OH$	$CH_3CH_2\overset{\overset{O}{\|\|}}{C}-OH$ propanoic acid
ester	$-\overset{\overset{O}{\|\|}}{C}-O-$	$R-\overset{\overset{O}{\|\|}}{C}-O-R'$	$CH_3CH_2\overset{\overset{O}{\|\|}}{C}OCH_3$ methyl propanoate
amine	$-\overset{\|}{N}-$	$R-\overset{\overset{R'}{\|}}{N}-R''$	$CH_3CH_2CH_2NH_2$ 1-propanamine
amide	$-\overset{\overset{O}{\|\|}}{C}-\overset{\|}{N}H$	$R-\overset{\overset{O}{\|\|}}{C}-\overset{\overset{R'}{\|}}{N}H$	$CH_3CH_2\overset{\overset{O}{\|\|}}{C}-NH_2$ propanamide

R represents a bonded atom or group of atoms.

Note: *R* represents a bonded atom or group of atoms.

Periodic Table of the Elements

KEY

Atomic Mass →	12.011	−4 +2 +4	← Selected Oxidation States
Symbol →	C		
Atomic Number →	6		
Electron Configuration →	2-4		

Relative atomic masses are based on $^{12}C = 12$ (exact)

Note: Numbers in parentheses are mass numbers of the most stable or common isotope.

Each cell: atomic mass, symbol, atomic number, electron configuration, selected oxidation states.

Period	Group 1	2	3	4	5	6	7	8	9	10	11	12	13	14	15	16	17	18
1	1.00794 **H** 1 1 +1 −1																	4.00260 **He** 2 2 0
2	6.941 **Li** 3 2-1 +1	9.01218 **Be** 4 2-2 +2											10.81 **B** 5 2-3 +3	12.011 **C** 6 2-4 −4 +2 +4	14.0067 **N** 7 2-5 −3 −2 −1 +1 +2 +3 +4 +5	15.9994 **O** 8 2-6 −2	18.9984 **F** 9 2-7 −1	20.180 **Ne** 10 2-8 0
3	22.98977 **Na** 11 2-8-1 +1	24.305 **Mg** 12 2-8-2 +2											26.98154 **Al** 13 2-8-3 +3	28.0855 **Si** 14 2-8-4 −4 +2 +4	30.97376 **P** 15 2-8-5 −3 +3 +5	32.065 **S** 16 2-8-6 −2 +4 +6	35.453 **Cl** 17 2-8-7 −1 +1 +5 +7	39.948 **Ar** 18 2-8-8 0
4	39.0983 **K** 19 2-8-8-1 +1	40.08 **Ca** 20 2-8-8-2 +2	44.9559 **Sc** 21 2-8-9-2 +3	47.867 **Ti** 22 2-8-10-2 +2 +3 +4	50.9415 **V** 23 2-8-11-2 +2 +3 +4 +5	51.996 **Cr** 24 2-8-13-1 +2 +3 +6	54.9380 **Mn** 25 2-8-13-2 +2 +3 +4 +7	55.845 **Fe** 26 2-8-14-2 +2 +3	58.9332 **Co** 27 2-8-15-2 +2 +3	58.693 **Ni** 28 2-8-16-2 +2 +3	63.546 **Cu** 29 2-8-18-1 +1 +2	65.409 **Zn** 30 2-8-18-2 +2	69.723 **Ga** 31 2-8-18-3 +3	72.64 **Ge** 32 2-8-18-4 +2 +4	74.9216 **As** 33 2-8-18-5 −3 +3 +5	78.96 **Se** 34 2-8-18-6 −2 +4 +6	79.904 **Br** 35 2-8-18-7 −1 +1 +5	83.798 **Kr** 36 2-8-18-8 0 +2
5	85.4678 **Rb** 37 2-8-18-8-1 +1	87.62 **Sr** 38 2-8-18-8-2 +2	88.9059 **Y** 39 2-8-18-9-2 +3	91.224 **Zr** 40 2-8-18-10-2 +4	92.9064 **Nb** 41 2-8-18-12-1 +3 +5	95.94 **Mo** 42 2-8-18-13-1 +6	(98) **Tc** 43 2-8-18-13-2 +4 +6 +7	101.07 **Ru** 44 2-8-18-15-1 +3	102.906 **Rh** 45 2-8-18-16-1 +3	106.42 **Pd** 46 2-8-18-18 +2 +4	107.868 **Ag** 47 2-8-18-18-1 +1	112.41 **Cd** 48 2-8-18-18-2 +2	114.818 **In** 49 2-8-18-18-3 +3	118.71 **Sn** 50 2-8-18-18-4 +2 +4	121.760 **Sb** 51 2-8-18-18-5 −3 +3 +5	127.60 **Te** 52 2-8-18-18-6 −2 +4 +6	126.904 **I** 53 2-8-18-18-7 −1 +1 +5 +7	131.29 **Xe** 54 2-8-18-18-8 0 +2 +4 +6
6	132.905 **Cs** 55 2-8-18-18-8-1 +1	137.33 **Ba** 56 2-8-18-18-8-2 +2	138.9055 **La** 57 2-8-18-18-9-2 +3	178.49 **Hf** 72 *18-32-10-2 +4	180.948 **Ta** 73 -18-32-11-2 +5	183.84 **W** 74 -18-32-12-2 +6	186.207 **Re** 75 -18-32-13-2 +4 +6 +7	190.23 **Os** 76 -18-32-14-2 +3 +4	192.217 **Ir** 77 -18-32-15-2 +3 +4	195.08 **Pt** 78 -18-32-17-1 +2 +4	196.967 **Au** 79 -18-32-18-1 +1 +3	200.59 **Hg** 80 -18-32-18-2 +1 +2	204.383 **Tl** 81 -18-32-18-3 +1 +3	207.2 **Pb** 82 -18-32-18-4 +2 +4	208.980 **Bi** 83 -18-32-18-5 +3 +5	(209) **Po** 84 -18-32-18-6 +2 +4	(210) **At** 85 -18-32-18-7	(222) **Rn** 86 -18-32-18-8 0
7	(223) **Fr** 87 -18-32-18-8-1 +1	(226) **Ra** 88 -18-32-18-8-2 +2	(227) **Ac** 89 -18-32-18-9-2 +3	(261) **Rf** 104 +4	(262) **Db** 105	(266) **Sg** 106	(272) **Bh** 107	(277) **Hs** 108	(276) **Mt** 109	(281) **Ds** 110	(280) **Rg** 111	(285) **Cn** 112	(284) **Uut** 113**	(289) **Uuq** 114	(288) **Uup** 115	(292) **Uuh** 116	(?) **Uus** 117	(294) **Uuo** 118

140.116 **Ce** 58 +3 +4	140.908 **Pr** 59 +3	144.24 **Nd** 60 +3	(145) **Pm** 61 +3	150.36 **Sm** 62 +2 +3	151.964 **Eu** 63 +2 +3	157.25 **Gd** 64 +3	158.925 **Tb** 65 +3	162.500 **Dy** 66 +3	164.930 **Ho** 67 +3	167.259 **Er** 68 +3	168.934 **Tm** 69 +3	173.04 **Yb** 70 +2 +3	174.9668 **Lu** 71 +3
232.038 **Th** 90 +4	231.036 **Pa** 91 +4 +5	238.029 **U** 92 +3 +4 +5 +6	(237) **Np** 93 +3 +4 +5 +6	(244) **Pu** 94 +3 +4 +5 +6	(243) **Am** 95 +3 +4 +5 +6	(247) **Cm** 96 +3	(247) **Bk** 97 +3 +4	(251) **Cf** 98 +3	(252) **Es** 99 +3	(257) **Fm** 100 +3	(258) **Md** 101 +2 +3	(259) **No** 102 +2 +3	(262) **Lr** 103 +3

*denotes the presence of (2-8-) for elements 72 and above

**The systematic names and symbols for elements of atomic numbers 113 and above will be used until the approval of trivial names by IUPAC.

Source: *CRC Handbook of Chemistry and Physics*, 91st ed., 2010–2011, CRC Press

Table S
Properties of Selected Elements

Atomic Number	Symbol	Name	First Ionization Energy (kJ/mol)	Electro-negativity	Melting Point (K)	Boiling* Point (K)	Density** (g/cm^3)	Atomic Radius (pm)
1	H	hydrogen	1312	2.2	14	20.	0.000082	32
2	He	helium	2372	—	—	4	0.000164	37
3	Li	lithium	520.	1.0	454	1615	0.534	130.
4	Be	beryllium	900.	1.6	1560.	2744	1.85	99
5	B	boron	801	2.0	2348	4273	2.34	84
6	C	carbon	1086	2.6	—	—	—	75
7	N	nitrogen	1402	3.0	63	77	0.001145	71
8	O	oxygen	1314	3.4	54	90.	0.001308	64
9	F	fluorine	1681	4.0	53	85	0.001553	60.
10	Ne	neon	2081	—	24	27	0.000825	62
11	Na	sodium	496	0.9	371	1156	0.97	160.
12	Mg	magnesium	738	1.3	923	1363	1.74	140.
13	Al	aluminum	578	1.6	933	2792	2.70	124
14	Si	silicon	787	1.9	1687	3538	2.3296	114
15	P	phosphorus (white)	1012	2.2	317	554	1.823	109
16	S	sulfur (monoclinic)	1000.	2.6	388	718	2.00	104
17	Cl	chlorine	1251	3.2	172	239	0.002898	100.
18	Ar	argon	1521	—	84	87	0.001633	101
19	K	potassium	419	0.8	337	1032	0.89	200.
20	Ca	calcium	590.	1.0	1115	1757	1.54	174
21	Sc	scandium	633	1.4	1814	3109	2.99	159
22	Ti	titanium	659	1.5	1941	3560.	4.506	148
23	V	vanadium	651	1.6	2183	3680.	6.0	144
24	Cr	chromium	653	1.7	2180.	2944	7.15	130.
25	Mn	manganese	717	1.6	1519	2334	7.3	129
26	Fe	iron	762	1.8	1811	3134	7.87	124
27	Co	cobalt	760.	1.9	1768	3200.	8.86	118
28	Ni	nickel	737	1.9	1728	3186	8.90	117
29	Cu	copper	745	1.9	1358	2835	8.96	122
30	Zn	zinc	906	1.7	693	1180.	7.134	120.
31	Ga	gallium	579	1.8	303	2477	5.91	123
32	Ge	germanium	762	2.0	1211	3106	5.3234	120.
33	As	arsenic (gray)	944	2.2	1090.	—	5.75	120.
34	Se	selenium (gray)	941	2.6	494	958	4.809	118
35	Br	bromine	1140.	3.0	266	332	3.1028	117
36	Kr	krypton	1351	—	116	120.	0.003425	116
37	Rb	rubidium	403	0.8	312	961	1.53	215
38	Sr	strontium	549	1.0	1050.	1655	2.64	190.
39	Y	yttrium	600.	1.2	1795	3618	4.47	176
40	Zr	zirconium	640.	1.3	2128	4682	6.52	164

Atomic Number	Symbol	Name	First Ionization Energy (kJ/mol)	Electro-negativity	Melting Point (K)	Boiling* Point (K)	Density** (g/cm^3)	Atomic Radius (pm)
41	Nb	niobium	652	1.6	2750.	5017	8.57	156
42	Mo	molybdenum	684	2.2	2896	4912	10.2	146
43	Tc	technetium	702	2.1	2430.	4538	11	138
44	Ru	ruthenium	710.	2.2	2606	4423	12.1	136
45	Rh	rhodium	720.	2.3	2237	3968	12.4	134
46	Pd	palladium	804	2.2	1828	3236	12.0	130.
47	Ag	silver	731	1.9	1235	2435	10.5	136
48	Cd	cadmium	868	1.7	594	1040.	8.69	140.
49	In	indium	558	1.8	430.	2345	7.31	142
50	Sn	tin (white)	709	2.0	505	2875	7.287	140.
51	Sb	antimony (gray)	831	2.1	904	1860.	6.68	140.
52	Te	tellurium	869	2.1	723	1261	6.232	137
53	I	iodine	1008	2.7	387	457	4.933	136
54	Xe	xenon	1170.	2.6	161	165	0.005366	136
55	Cs	cesium	376	0.8	302	944	1.873	238
56	Ba	barium	503	0.9	1000.	2170.	3.62	206
57	La	lanthanum	538	1.1	1193	3737	6.15	194
			Elements 58–71 have been omitted.					
72	Hf	hafnium	659	1.3	2506	4876	13.3	164
73	Ta	tantalum	728	1.5	3290.	5731	16.4	158
74	W	tungsten	759	1.7	3695	5828	19.3	150.
75	Re	rhenium	756	1.9	3458	5869	20.8	141
76	Os	osmium	814	2.2	3306	5285	22.587	136
77	Ir	iridium	865	2.2	2719	4701	22.562	132
78	Pt	platinum	864	2.2	2041	4098	21.5	130.
79	Au	gold	890.	2.4	1337	3129	19.3	130.
80	Hg	mercury	1007	1.9	234	630.	13.5336	132
81	Tl	thallium	589	1.8	577	1746	11.8	144
82	Pb	lead	716	1.8	600.	2022	11.3	145
83	Bi	bismuth	703	1.9	544	1837	9.79	150.
84	Po	polonium	812	2.0	527	1235	9.20	142
85	At	astatine	—	2.2	575	—	—	148
86	Rn	radon	1037	—	202	211	0.009074	146
87	Fr	francium	393	0.7	300.	—	—	242
88	Ra	radium	509	0.9	969	—	5	211
89	Ac	actinium	499	1.1	1323	3471	10.	201
			Elements 90 and above have been omitted.					

*boiling point at standard pressure

**density of solids and liquids at room temperature and density of gases at 298 K and 101.3 kPa

— no data available

Table T
Important Formulas and Equations

Density	$d = \frac{m}{V}$	d = density m = mass V = volume
Mole Calculations	$\text{number of moles} = \frac{\text{given mass}}{\text{gram-formula mass}}$	
Percent Error	$\%\ \text{error} = \frac{\text{measured value} - \text{accepted value}}{\text{accepted value}} \times 100$	
Percent Composition	$\%\ \text{composition by mass} = \frac{\text{mass of part}}{\text{mass of whole}} \times 100$	
Concentration	$\text{parts per million} = \frac{\text{mass of solute}}{\text{mass of solution}} \times 1\,000\,000$	
	$\text{molarity} = \frac{\text{moles of solute}}{\text{liter of solution}}$	
Combined Gas Law	$\frac{P_1V_1}{T_1} = \frac{P_2V_2}{T_2}$	P = pressure V = volume T = temperature
Titration	$M_AV_A = M_BV_B$	M_A = molarity of H^+ M_B = molarity of OH^- V_A = volume of acid V_B = volume of base
Heat	$q = mC\Delta T$ $q = mH_f$ $q = mH_v$	q = heat H_f = heat of fusion m = mass H_v = heat of vaporization C = specific heat capacity ΔT = change in temperature
Temperature	$K = °C + 273$	K = kelvin °C = degree Celsius

NOTE: Important decay equations below *are not* parts of the new 2011 Reference Table Edition.

Radioactive Decay	$\text{fraction remaining} = \left(\frac{1}{2}\right)^{\frac{t}{T}}$ $\text{number of half-life periods} = \frac{t}{T}$	t = total time elapsed T = half-life

Chemistry Terms

A

Absolute Zero
0K or -273°C; the temperature at which all molecular movements stop.

Accelerator
a device which gives charged particles sufficient kinetic energy to penetrate the nucleus.

Acetylene (see ethyne)

Acid, Arrhenius
a substance that produces H+ (hydrogen ion, proton) or H_3O^+ (hydronium) ion as the positive ion is solutions.

Acid , Alternate Theory
a substance that donates H+ (hydrogen ion, proton) in acids-base reactions.

Activated complex
a high energy substance formed during a chemical reaction

Activation energy
minimal amount of energy needed to start a reaction.

Addition reaction
organic reaction that involves the adding of hydrogen atoms (or halogen atoms) to a double or a triple bond.

Addition polymerization
the joining of monomers (small unit molecules) with double bonds to form a polymer (a larger unit) molecule.

Alcohol
an organic compound containing the hydroxyl group (-OH) as a functional group.

Aldehyde
an organic compound containing the $-\overset{\overset{O}{\|}}{C}-H$ as the functional group.

Alkali metal
an element in Group 1 of the Periodic Table.

Alkaline Earth metal
an element in Group 2 of the Periodic Table.

Alkalinity
describes how basic is a solution

Alkane
a saturated hydrocarbon with all single bonds and a general formula of C_nH_{2n+2}

Alkene
an unsaturated hydrocarbon with a double bond and a general formula of C_nH_{2n}

Alkyl group
a hydrocarbon group (found as a side chain) that contains one less H atom than an alkane with the same number of C atoms.

Alkyne
an unsaturated hydrocarbon with a triple (≡) bond and a general formula of C_nH_{2n-2}

Aldehyde
organic compound containing $-\overset{O}{\overset{\|}{C}}-H$

Allotropes
two or more different forms of the same element that have different formulas, structures, and properties.

Alpha decay
a nuclear decay that releases an alpha particle.

Alpha particle
a helium nuclei, $^{4}_{2}He$

Amide
an organic compound formed from a reaction of organic acid with an amine.

Amine
an organic compound that has $-\overset{|}{N}-$ (nitrogen) as its functional group.

Amino acid
an organic compound containing an amine ($-NH_2-$) and a carboxyl ($-COOH$) group.

Anode
an electrode (site) where oxidation occurs in electrochemical (voltaic and electrolytic) cells. In voltaic cells, the anode is negative. In electrolytic cells, the anode is positive.

Aqueous solutions
a homogeneous mixture made with water as the solvent.

Artificial Transmutation
converting (transforming) a stable element to a radioactive unstable element by bombarding (hitting) the stable nucleus with a high energy particle.

Asymmetrical molecule
a molecule that has a polarized structure because of an uneven charge distribution.

Atom
the basic or the smallest unit of an element that can be involved in chemical reactions.

Atomic mass
the weighted average mass of an element's naturally occurring isotopes.

Atomic mass unit
one-twelfth ($1/12^{th}$) the mass of a carbon-12 atom.

Atomic number
the number of protons in the nucleus of an atom.

Atomic radius (size)
half the distance between adjacent nuclei of identical bonded atoms.

Avogadro's law (hypothesis)
equal volume of all gases under the same pressure and temperature contain equal number of molecules.

Avogadro's number
quantity of particles in one mole of a substance; 6.02×10^{23}

B

Base, Arrhenius
a substance that produces OH- (hydroxide) ion as the only negative ion in solutions.

Base, Alternate Theory
a substance that accepts H+ (hydrogen ion, protons) in acid-base reactions.

Battery
an electrochemical (voltaic) cell that produces electricity from a redox reaction.

Beta particle
a high-speed electron , $^{0}_{-1}e$, released from atomic nucleus during a nuclear decay.

Beta decay
a nuclear decay that releases a beta particle.

Binary compound
a chemical substance composed of two different elements chemically combined.

Boiling point
the temperature of a liquid at which the vapor pressure of the liquid is equal to the atmospheric pressure. Boiling point of water = 100°C

Boyle's Law
describes behavior of a gas at constant temperature: At constant temperature, volume of a gas varies indirectly with the pressure.

Bronsted-Lowry acid and bases (see alternate theory)

C

Calorimeter
a device used in measuring heat energy change during a physical and a chemical process.

Catalyst
a substance that speeds up a reaction by providing an alternate, lower activation energy pathway.

Cathode
an electrode (site) where reduction occurs in electrochemical cell.
In Voltaic cells, the cathode is Positive. In Electrolytic cells, the cathode is Negative.

Charles' Law
describes behavior of gases at constant pressure: at constant pressure, the volume of a gas is directly proportional to its Kelvin (absolute) temperature.

Chemical bonding
the simultaneous attraction of two nuclei to electrons.

Chemical change
the changing of compositions of one or more substances during chemical reactions.

Chemical formula
expression of qualitative and quantitative composition of pure substances.

Chemical property
a characteristic of a substance based on its interaction with other substances.

Chemistry
the study of the composition, properties, changes, and energy of matter.

Coefficient
a number (usually a whole number) in front of a formula that indicates how many moles (or unit) of that substance.

Collision Theory
for a chemical reaction to occur, reacting particles must collide effectively.

Combined gas law

Combustion
an exothermic reaction of a substance with oxygen to release energy.

Compound
a substance composed of two or more different elements chemically combined in a definite ratio
a substance that can be separated (decomposed) only by chemical methods.

Concentrated solution
a solution containing large amount of dissolved solute relative to amount of solvent.

Condensation
exothermic phase change of a substance from gas (vapor) to a liquid.

Condensation polymerization
the joining of monomers (small unit molecules) into a polymer (a large unit molecule) by the removal of water.

Conductivity
ability of an electrical current to flow through a substance.
conductivity of electrolytes (soluble substances) in aqueous and liquid phase is due to mobile ions. Conductivity of metallic substances is due to mobile valance electrons.

Coordinate covalent bond
a type of covalent bond in which one atom provides both shared electrons with H+

Covalent bond
a bond formed by the sharing of electrons between nonmetal atoms.

Cracking
the breaking of a large hydrocarbon molecule into smaller molecules.

Crystallization
a process of recovering a solute from a solution (mixture) by evaporation (or boiling).

D

Dalton's law of partial pressure
total pressure of a gas mixture is the sum of all the individual gas pressures

Decomposition
chemical reaction in which a compound is broken down into simpler substances.

Density
mass per unit volume of a substance ; Density = $\frac{\text{mass}}{\text{volume}}$

Deposition
an exothermic phase change by which a gas changes to a solid.

Diatomic molecules (element)
a molecule consisting of two identical atoms.

Dihydroxyl alcohol
an alcohol with two –OH groups

Dilute solution
a solution containing little dissolved solute in comparison to the amount of solvent.

Dipole (aka polar)
a molecule with positive and negative ends due to uneven charge distributions.

Distillation
a process by which components of a homogeneous mixture can be separated by differences in boiling points.

Double covalent bond (=)
the sharing of two pairs of electrons (four total electrons) between two atoms.

Double replacement
a chemical reaction that involves the exchange of ions.

Ductile
ability (property) of a metal to be drawn into a thin wire.

E

Effective collision
a collision in which the particles collide with sufficient kinetic energy, and at appropriate angle.

Electrochemical cell
a system in which there is a flow of electrical current while a chemical reaction is taking place. Voltaic and Electrolytic cells are the two most common types of electrochemical cells.

Electrode
a site at which oxidation or reduction can occur in electrochemical cells. Anode (Oxidation site) and Cathode (Reduction site) are two electrodes of electrochemical cells.

Electrolysis
a process by which electrical current forces a nonspontaneous redox reaction to occur.
Electrolysis of water: $2H_2O$ + electricity -------> $2\,H_2$ + O_2

Electrolyte
a substances that dissolves in water to produce an aqueous solution that which conducts electricity. Conductivity of an electrolyte is due to mobile ions in solutions.

Electrolytic cell
an electrochemical cell that requires an electrical current to cause a nonspontaneous redox reaction to occur.

Electron
a negatively charge subatomic particle found surrounding the nucleus (in orbital) of an atom.

Electron configuration
distribution of electrons in electron shells (energy levels) of an atom.

Electron-dot diagram
a diagram showing the symbol of an atom and dots equal to the number of valance electrons.

Electronegativity
a measure of atom's ability (tendency) to attract electrons during chemical bonding.

Electrolytic reduction
the use of electrolytic cell to force an ion to gain electrons and form a neutral atom.

Electroplating
use of electrolytic cell to coat a thin layer of a metal into another surface.

Element
a substance composed of atoms of the same atomic number.
a substance that cannot be decomposed (broken down) into simpler substances.

Empirical formula
a formula showing atoms combined in the simplest whole number ratio.

Empty space theory
Rutherford's gold foil experimental conclusion that atom is mostly empty space.

Endothermic
a process that absorbs energy.
Products of endothermic reaction always have more energy than the reactants.

Energy
ability to do work; can be measured in joules or calories.

Entropy
a measure of the disorder or randomness of a system.
entropy increases from solid to liquid to gas and with increase in temperature

Equilibrium
a state of a system when the rates (speed) of opposing processes (reaction) are equal.

Ester
an organic compound with $-\overset{\displaystyle O}{\overset{\|}{C}}-O$ (–COO–) as the functional group.

Esterification
an organic reaction between an alcohol and organic acid to produce an ester.

Ether
an organic compound with – O – as the functional group.

Ethene (Ethylene)
first member of the alkene hydrocarbons with a formula of C_2H_4

H \ / H
C = C
H / \ H

Ethyne (acetylene)
first member of the alkyne hydrocarbons with formula of C_2H_2 $H-C\equiv C-H$

Evaporation
an endothermic phase change by which a liquid changes to gas (vapor)

Excited state
a state of an atom in which electrons are at higher electron shells (energy levels)

Exothermic
a process that releases energy.
Products of exothermic reactions always have less energy than the reactants.

F

Family (Group)
vertical column of the Periodic Table.
elements in the same family have same number of valance electrons and share similar chemical properties.

Fermentation
an organic reaction in which sugar is converted to alcohol (ethanol, C_2H_5OH) and carbon dioxide.

Filtration
a process that is used to separate a liquid mixture that is composed of substances with different particle sizes.

Fission
the splitting of a large nucleus into smaller nuclei fragment in a nuclear reaction.
mass is converted to huge amounts of energy during fission.

Formula
symbols and subscripts used to represent the composition of a substance.

Formula mass
total mass of all the atoms in one unit of formula.

Freezing (solidification)
an exothermic phase change by which a liquid changes to a solid.

Freezing point (solid/liquid equilibrium)
the temperature at which both solid and liquid phases of a substance can exist at equilibrium the freezing point and melting point of a substance are the same.

Functional group
an atom or a group of atoms that replaces a hydrogen atom in a hydrocarbon .

Fusion (nuclear change)
the joining of two small nuclei to make a larger nucleus in a nuclear reaction.

Fusion (melting) phase change
endothermic phase change by which a solid changes to liquid.

G

Gamma ray
high-energy rays similar to X-ray that is released during nuclear decay.
a gamma ray has zero mass and zero charge $^{0}_{0}\gamma$

Gaseous phase
a phase of matter with no definite shape and no definite volume.

Gay-Lussac's law
at constant volume, pressure of a gas varies directly with the Kelvin temperature

Geological dating
determining the age of a rock or mineral by comparing amounts of Uranium-238 to Lead-206 in a sample.

Gram-formula mass
a mass of one mole of a substance expressed in grams.
the total mass of all atoms in one mole of a substance.

Ground state
a state of an atom in which all electrons of the atom occupy the lowest available levels.

Group (family)
the vertical column of the Periodic Table.
elements in the same group have the same number of valance electrons and share similar chemical properties.

H

Haber process
a chemical reaction that produces ammonia from nitrogen and hydrogen.
N_2 + $3H_2$ ----------> $2NH_3$ (Haber process equation).

Half-life
the length of time it takes for a sample of a radioisotope to decay to half its original mass (or atoms

Half-reaction
a reaction that shows either the oxidation or the reduction part of a redox reaction.

Halide
a compound that contains a halogen (Group 17) atom.

Halogen
an element found in Group 17 of the Periodic Table.

Heat
a form of energy that can flow (or transfer) from one substance (or area) to another.
Joules and calories are two units commonly used to measure the quantity of heat.

Heat of fusion
the amount of heat needed to change a unit mass of a solid to a liquid at its melting point.. Heat of fusion for water is 334 Joules per gram.

Heat of reaction (ΔH)
amount of heat absorbed or released during a reaction.
the difference between the heat energy of the products and the heat energy of the reactants. **ΔH** = heat of products – heat of reactants.

Heat of vaporization
the amount of heat needed to change a unit mass of a liquid to vapor (gas) at its boiling point. Heat of vaporization for water is 2260 Joules per gram.

Heterogeneous
a mixture in which substances in the mixture are not uniformly or evenly mixed.

Homogeneous
a type of mixture in which substances in the mixture are uniformly and evenly mixed. Solutions are homogenous mixtures.

Homologous series
a group of related compounds in which one member differs from the next member by a set number of atoms.

Hydrate
an ionic compound containing a set number of water molecules within its crystal structures. $CuSO_4 \cdot 5H_2O$ is an example formula of a hydrate. This hydrate contains five moles of water.

Hydrocarbon
an organic compound containing only hydrogen and carbon atoms.

Hydrogen bonding
attraction of a hydrogen atom to oxygen, nitrogen, or fluorine atom of another molecule. Hydrogen bonding exists (or is strongest) in H_2O (water) , NH_3 (ammonia), and HF (hydrogen fluoride).

Hydrogen ion (H^+)
a hydrogen atom that had lost its only electron. H+ is similar to a proton. the only positive ion produced by all Arrhenius acids in solutions.

Hydrolysis
a reaction of a salt in water to produce either an acidic, a basic, or neutral solution.

Hydronium ion (H_3O^+)
a polyatomic ion formed when H_2O (a water molecule) combines with H^+ (hydrogen ion). ion formed by all Arrhenius acids in solutions.

Hydroxide ion (OH^-)
the only negative ion produced by Arrhenius bases in solutions.

Hydroxyl group (–OH)
a functional group found in compounds of alcohols.

I

Ideal gas
a theoretical gas that posses all the characteristics described by the kinetic molecular theory

Immiscible liquids
two liquids that do not mix well with each other

Indicator
any substance that change color in the presence of a another substance.
acid-base indicators are used to determine if a substance is an acid or a base.

Inert gas (noble gas)
elements in Group 18 of the Periodic Table.

Insoluble
a solute substance with low solubility (doesn't dissolve well) in a given solvent.

Intermolecular forces
weak force of attraction between molecules of molecular substances in liquid and solid phase

Ion
a charged (+ or -) particle

Ionic bond
a bond formed by the transfer of one or more electrons from a metal to a nonmetal.
An ionic bond is formed by electrostatic attraction of positive ion to a negative ion.

Ionic compound (substance)
compounds that are composed of positive and negative particles.
NaCl, $LiNO_3$, and ammonium chloride are examples of ionic substances.

Ionic radius
the size of an ion as measured from the nucleus to the outer energy level of that ion.

Ionization energy
energy needed to remove the most loosely bound valance electrons from an atom.

Isomers
organic compounds with the same molecular formula but different structural formulas.

Isotopes
atoms of the same element with the same number of protons but different number of neutrons. Isotopes have same atomic number but different mass numbers.

J - K

Joules
a unit for measuring the amount of heat energy.

Kelvin (K)
a unit for measuring temperature. A Kelvin temperature unit is always 273 higher than the equivalent temperature in Celsius. $K = {}^{o}C + 273$

Ketone
an organic compound containing $-\overset{O}{\overset{||}{C}}-$ or –CO –), a carbonyl functional group

Kinetic energy
energy due to motion or movement of particles in a substance.
average kinetic energy of particles determines temperature of a substance.

Kinetic molecular theory (ideal gas law)
a theory that is used to explain behavior of gas particles.

Kinetics
the study of rates and mechanisms of reactions

L

Law of conservation
a chemical reaction mass, atoms, charges, and energy are conserved (neither created nor destroyed).

Law of definite proportion
atoms of a compound are in a fixed ratio.

Le Chatelier's principle
a chemical or physical process will shift at equilibrium to compensate for added stress

Lewis electron-dot diagram
a diagram showing the symbol of an atom and dots equal to the number of its valance electrons.

Liquid
a phase of matter with definite volume but no definite shape (takes the shape of the container).

Luster
a property that describes the shininess of a metallic element

M

Malleability
ability (or property) of a metal to be hammered into a thin sheet.
the total number of protons and neutrons in the nucleus of an atom.

Matter
anything that has mass and volume (occupied space).

Melting point (solid/liquid equilibrium)
the temperature at which both the solid and the liquid phases of a substance can co-exist. The melting point of water is 0°C or 273 K.

Metal
an element that tend to lose electrons and form a positive ion during chemical reactions. Majority of the elements (about 75%) are metals.

Metallic bond
bonding in metals described as "positive ions immersed in a sea of mobile electrons"

Metalloid
an element with both metallic and nonmetallic properties (characteristics).

Mixture
a physical combination of two or more substances that can be homogeneous or heterogeneous. Mixtures can be separated by physical methods.

Molar mass
mass in grams of one mole of a formula

Molar volume
volume of one mole of a gas at STP is equal to 22.4 liters

Molarity
concentration of a solution expressed in moles of solute per liter of solution.

$$\text{Molarity} = \frac{\text{moles of solute}}{\text{liter of solution}}$$

Mole
unit of quantity of particles (atoms, molecule, ions, electrons) in a substance
1 mole = 6.02 x 10^{23} particles

Molecular formula
a formula showing the actual composition (or ratio of atoms) in a substance

Molecule
the smallest unit of a covalent (molecular) substance that has the same properties of the substance.
a molecule could be one nonmetal atom (He, Ne) or a group of nonmetal atoms ($C_6H_{12}O_6$, HCl, H_2O) covalently bonded

Molecular substance (covalent substance)
a substance composed of molecules
H_2O CO_2 O_2 NH_3 $C_6H_{12}O_6$ are examples of molecular substances.

Monomer
an individual unit of a polymer.

Multiple covalent bond
a double or a triple covalent bond formed by the sharing of more than two electrons.

N

Network solid bond
covalent bonding with absent of discrete particles in network solid substances

Neutralization
a reaction of an acid with a base to produce water and salt.

Neutron
a subatomic particle with no charge found in the nucleus of an atom

Noble gas (inert gas)
an element found in Group 18 of the Periodic Table

Nonmetal
an element that tends to gain electrons and forms negative ions, or shares electrons to form a covalent bond.

Nonpolar covalent bond
a bond formed by the equal sharing of electrons between two identical atoms (or of the same electronegativity)

Nonpolar substance
a substance whose molecules have symmetrical shape and even charge distribution

Nucleons
particles in the nucleus that includes protons and neutrons

Nucleus
the small, dense, positive core of an atom containing protons and neutrons.

O

Octet rule
when an atom has a stable configuration with eight electrons in the valance shell.

Orbital
a region in an atom where electrons are likely to be found (or located).

Orbital notation
a diagram showing arrangements of electrons in orbitals of atoms

Organic acid
a compound containing $-COOH$ or $\overset{O}{\overset{\|}{C}} - OH$ as its functional group.

Organic chemistry
the study of carbon and carbon based compounds.

Oxidation
the loss of electrons by an atom during a redox reaction.
oxidation leads to an increase in oxidation state (number) of a substance.

Oxidized substance (Reducing agent)
a substance that loss electrons in a redox reaction.
a substance whose oxidation number (state) increases after a redox reaction

Oxidizing agent (Reduced substance)
a substance that is reduced (gained electrons) in a redox reaction.
a substance whose oxidation number (state) decreases after a redox reaction

Oxidation number/ Oxidation state
a charge an atom has or appears to have during a redox reaction

Ozone
O_3, an allotrope (a different molecular form) of oxygen

P

Parts per million
concentration of a solution expressed as ratio of grams of solute per million parts of a solution.

$$\text{Part per million (ppm)} = \frac{\text{grams of solute}}{\text{grams of solution}} \times 1\,000\,000$$

Percent composition
composition of a compound as the percentage by mass of each element compared to the total mass of the compound.

$$\text{Percent composition} = \frac{\text{mass of part}}{\text{mass of whole}} \times 100$$

Period
the horizontal row of the Periodic Table
elements in a period have the same number of occupied electron shells (or energy levels

Periodic law
states that properties of elements are periodic functions of their atomic numbers.

pH
values that indicate the strength of an acid or a base. pH values ranges from 1 – 14.
pH values is determined from how much H^+ ions are in a solution.

Phase change diagram
a diagram showing changes in a substances as it is being heated or cooling over time

Phase equilibrium
a state of balance when the rates of two opposing (opposite) phase changes are equal.

Physical change
a change that does not change the composition of a substance.
phase change and dissolving are examples of physical changes.

Physical properties
characteristics of a substance that can be observed or measured without changing the chemical composition of the substance

Polar covalent bond
a bond formed by the unequal sharing of electrons between two different nonmetal atoms.

Polyatomic ion
group of two or more atoms with excess positive or negative charge (See Table E).

Polymer
an organic compound composed of chains of monomers (smaller units).

Polymerization
an organic reaction by which monomers (small units molecules) are joined together to make a polymer (a larger unit molecule) .

Position (electron catcher)
a positively charge particle similar in mass to an electron. $^{0}_{+1}e$

Positron decay (emission)
a nuclear decay that releases a positron

Potential energy
stored energy in chemical substances.
amount of potential energy depends on composition and the structure of a substance.

Potential energy diagram
a diagram showing the changes in potential energy of substances during a reaction.

Precipitate
a solid that forms out of a solution

Primary alcohol
an alcohol with –OH functional group attached to an end carbon

Product
a substance that remained (or formed) after a chemical reaction is completed.
products are placed to the right of an arrow in equations.

Proton
a subatomic particle with a positive charge found in the nucleus of an atom.
the number of protons in an atom is equal to the atomic number of the element.

Pure substances
a type of matter with the same composition and properties in all samples.
elements and compounds are pure substances.

Q

Qualitative
indicates the types of atom that are in a chemical formula.

Quanta
specific amount of energy absorbed or released by an electron as it changes from one level to another.

Quantum theory
describes location and behavior of electrons in sets of four quantum numbers

Quantitative
indicates the number of each atom in a formula.

R

Radioisotope
an unstable isotope of an element that is radioactive and can decay.

Rate
a measure of the speed (how fast) a reaction occurs.

Reactant
the starting substance in a chemical reaction.
reactants are shown (or placed) to the left of the arrow in equations.

Redox
a reaction that involves oxidation and reduction.

Reduction
the gaining of electrons during a redox reaction.
reduction leads to a decrease in oxidation number (state) of a substance

Reduced substance (oxidizing agent)
a substance that gained electron during a redox reaction
a substance whose oxidation number (state) decreases after a reaction

Reducing agent (oxidized substance)
the substance that is oxidized (loss electrons) in a redox reaction.
a substance whose oxidation number (state) increases after a redox reaction.

S

Saponification
organic reaction that produces soap and glycerol (a trihydroxy alcohol).

Salt
a product of neutralization reaction.
an ionic substance.

Salt bridge
allows for ions to flow (migrate) between the two half cells of voltaic cells.

Saturated hydrocarbon
alkane hydrocarbon with only single bonds between the carbon atoms.

Saturated solution
a solution containing the maximum amount of dissolved solute possible at a given temperature.

Secondary alcohol
an alcohol in which the –OH is bonded to a carbon atom that is already bonded to two other carbon atoms.

Single covalent bond
a covalent bond formed by the sharing of just two electrons (or one pair of electrons)

Single replacement
a reaction in which a more reactive element replaces the less reactive element of a compound.

Solid
a phase of matter with definite shape and definite volume

Solubility
a measure of the extent to which a solute will dissolve in a given solvent at a specifiedtemperature.

Soluble
a substance with high solubility.

Solute
the substance that is being dissolved.
when a salt dissolves in water, the solute is the salt.

Solution
a homogeneous mixture of substances in the same physical state.

Solvent
the substance (usually a liquid) that is dissolving the solute.
water is the solvent in all aqueous solutions.

Specific heat capacity
amount of heat needed to change the temperature of a one gram sample of a substance by one ^{o}C

Spectral lines (bright-line spectrum)
band of colors produces as electron go from excited (high) to ground (low) state

Spontaneous reaction
a reaction that will occur under a given set of conditions
a reaction that proceed in the direction of lower energy and greater entropy

STP
standard temperature ($0^{o}C$, 273 K) and pressure (1 atm, 101.3 kPa)

Stress
a change in temperature, pressure, concentration to a reaction at equilibrium.

Sublimation
an endothermic phase change from solid to gas.

Subscript
a whole number written next to a chemical symbol to indicate ho many atoms

Substitution reaction
an organic reaction of an alkane with a halogen to produce a halide.
a reaction in which a halogen atom replaces a hydrogen atom of an alkane (saturated) hydrocarbon.

Supersaturated solution
a solution containing more solutes than would dissolve at that given temperature.

Symmetrical molecule
a molecule that has a nonpolarized structure due to an even charge distribution.

Synthesis
a chemical reaction in which two or more substances combine to make one substance.

T

Temperature
the measure of the average kinetic energy of particles in a substance
temperature and average kinetic energy are directly related.

Tertiary alcohol
an alcohol in which the –OH is bonded to a carbon atom that is already bonded to three other carbon atoms.

Thompson, JJ
conducted cathode ray experiment that lead to the discovery of electrons

Titration
a process used in determining the concentration of an unknown solution by reacting it with a solution of a known concentration.

Tracer
a radioisotope used to track a chemical reaction.

Transition element
an element found in Group 3 – 12 of the Periodic Table

Transmutation
the changing or converting of a nucleus of one atom into a nucleus of a different atom

Trihydroxy alcohol
an alcohol with three –OH (hydroxyl) groups

Triple covalent bond
a covalent bond resulting from the sharing of three pairs of electrons (six total electrons).

U - W

Unsaturated hydrocarbon
organic compound containing double or triple bonded carbon atoms.

Unsaturated solution
a solution containing less dissolved solute than can be dissolved at a given temperature

Valance electrons
the electrons in the outermost electron shell (energy level) of an atom.

Vapor
a gas form of a substance that is normally a liquid at room temperature

Vapor pressure
the pressure exerted by vapor (evaporated particles) on the surface of the liquid

Vaporization (evaporation)
phase change of a substance from liquid to a gaseous state at its boiling point.

Voltaic cell
an electrochemical cell in which electrical energy is produced from a spontaneous redox chemical reaction.

Wave-mechanical model (electron-cloud model)
the current model of an atom that places electrons in orbital.
the orbital is described as the probable location (region) of finding electrons in an

Review Book
Surviving Chemistry
One Concept at a Time
A Review of High School Chemistry Concepts
Excite Engage Enhance
e3Chemistry
Effiong Eyo
Student Name:
Teacher Name:
Period:
School Year:
Review Book
Surviving Chemistry
Student Answer Sheet Booklet
e3Chemistry
Effiong Eyo

Workbook
Surviving Chemistry
One Concept at a Time
A Workbook for High School Chemistry
(A companion to the Guided Study Book)
e3Chemistry
Guided Study Book
Surviving Chemistry
One Concept at a Time
A Guided Study book for High School Chemistry
(A companion to the Workbook)
e3Chemistry
Effiong Eyo

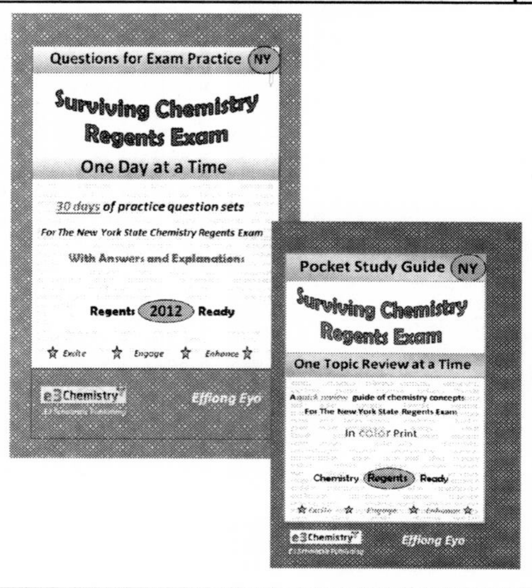
Questions for Exam Practice NY
Surviving Chemistry Regents Exam
One Day at a Time
30 days of practice question sets
For The New York State Chemistry Regents Exam
With Answers and Explanations
Regents 2012 Ready
Excite Engage Enhance
e3Chemistry
Effiong Eyo
Pocket Study Guide NY
Surviving Chemistry Regents Exam
One Topic Review at a Time
A quick review guide of chemistry concepts
For The New York State Regents Exam
In color Print
Chemistry Regents Ready
Excite Engage Enhance
e3Chemistry
Effiong Eyo

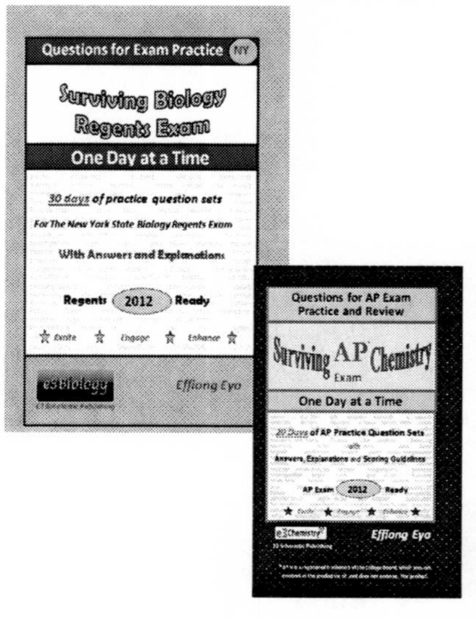
Questions for Exam Practice NY
Surviving Biology Regents Exam
One Day at a Time
30 days of practice question sets
For The New York State Biology Regents Exam
With Answers and Explanations
Regents 2012 Ready
Excite Engage Enhance
e3Biology
Effiong Eyo
Questions for AP Exam Practice and Review
Surviving AP Chemistry Exam
One Day at a Time
30 Days of AP Practice Question Sets
with Answers, Explanations and Scoring Guidelines
AP Exam 2012 Ready
Excite Engage Enhance
e3Chemistry
Effiong Eyo

School/Class order price per book . Prices reflect up 43% discount.

Review Book (black print)*	13.64
Review Book (color print)*	33.60
Review Book Student Answer Sheet Booklet	3.99
Workbook *	15.99
Guided Study Book (black print)*	15.99
Guided Study Book (color print)*	44.99
Questions for Chemistry Regents Exam Practice	13.64
Pocket Regents Study Guide (black print)	11.82
Pocket Regents Study Guide (color print)	19.98
Questions for Biology Regents Exam Practice	13.64
Questions for Chemistry AP Exam Practice	14.64

***Free Answer Key Booklet (up to 4 copies) for teachers with class order**

Online	Mail	Phone / Fax
e3chemistry.com	E3 Scholastic Publishing 7 MARNE AVE NEWBURGH, NY 12550	(877) 224 - 0487

We print and ship fast.

Most individual orders are shipped within 2 days.

Most class-size orders are shipped within 7 days.

Call us and we'll work with you and your school to get our exciting books to you and your students at additional discount.